perspectives on management systems approaches in education

perspectives on management systems approaches in education

a symposium

albert h. yee
editor

educational technology publications
englewood cliffs, new jersey 07632

Library of Congress Cataloging in Publication Data

Yee, Albert H
    Perspectives on management systems approaches in education.

    Expanded papers originally presented as a symposium held during the 1972 American Educational Research Association meeting, Chicago.
    1. School management and organization. 2. Performance contracts in education. I. Title.
LB2806.Y43   371.2   72-12729
ISBN 0-87778-044-7

Library of Congress Catalog Card Number: 72-12729.

International Standard Book Number: 0-87778-044-7.

First Printing.

PREFACE

In terms of fundamental principles and value orientations, certain frames of reference and practices have dominated curriculum development and school organization more than others. Today's school programs and methods stem largely from the rational/empirical/behavioral frame of reference, which induces pragmatic assumptions such that education can become a scientifically ordered enterprise and should develop definite curriculum and instruction that can stand the test of cost-effectiveness. All levels of education show increasingly greater commitment to larger, systematic organizations operating on the basis of management accountability and outcome evaluation as determined by research and development. Unanimity concerning the feasibility of the rational frame, especially among educational leaders and researchers, has become so complete that the great majority of educators offer little or no challenge to its pre-eminence and seldom pursue perspective.

However, conformity and lack of debate do not denote substantive knowledge and comprehension of how and why such practices should prevail. Most teachers and principals concern themselves very little with the substance and esoterica of empirical approaches, but they presume suffi-

73595

cient understanding about them to practice modern teaching concepts. As school organizations grow larger and more complex each year, the individual input of practitioners into policies and programs decreases and they must become more acquiescent to the specialized expertise and judgment of researchers and central administrators who determine educational opinions and decisions for them. Forming an elite structure, researchers and administrators tend to be managers and engineers, not theorists and philosophers; and many of them have never taught youngsters.

In this age of rising bureaucracy and scientific-economic-technological development, education has changed from a cottage industry which emphasized the master craftsman and personalized approaches to a formalized, institutionalized structure with differentiated staff roles and expectations. Such changes in America's participatory system of education would seem to require corresponding dialogue, cross-evaluation processes, and special efforts to decentralize responsibilities. Therefore, the leadership and organizational developments in professional education present a tremendous need for the greater explication of basic educational principles, especially in terms of the predominant rational approaches to today's problems.

The prevailing apathy concerning fundamental principles and values reflects in part the greater emphasis upon power, expedience, and politics in education in order to handle mounting exigencies, such as finances, shifting enrollments, disadvantaged groups, and teacher militancy for higher benefits. The rational frame of reference is appealing to most decision-makers, because it relates organizational and functional prediction and control, and generates practical answers and assessment modes contrary to the past dependence of educators upon subjective opinion and verbal slogans. However, while problem-solving is sought through a narrow *modus operandi*, the decision-maker is channeled to some degree by the solutions and direction of progress that his frame generates. Also, the rational frame and decision-making process lead practitioners to undertake programs and methods that they are not involved in developing, do not fully comprehend, and often perceive as one-sided and belittling. The superficial stress upon the mechanical and quantitative tends to put the practitioner more "in line" with the processes than in development and control of them and perceives learners as "manipulated" and conforming recipients instead of as interactive individuals.

There is a growing uneasiness in America (e.g., C.E. Silberman's *Crisis in the Classroom*) about the formulation and handling of educational policies and programs; and, unfortunately, many educators seem unaware that one basic source of the concern could well be the inadequate dialogue (or the attitude toward seeking dialogue) on fundamental principles in professional education. For example, the financial situation facing most school systems today seems to come from a lack of real school-community relations and over-reliance by schools upon a narrow quantitative frame of reference. It seems the problem at hand, therefore, becomes one of perspective and assessing what basic assumptions underlie curricular policies and programs, especially on the part of opinion-leaders and decision-makers in professional education.

Becoming more knowledgeable in technical methods and gadgetry is not what is needed to overcome the problems of perspective that must be confronted. Techniques and facilities in and of themselves do not create the problems we wish to discuss, for their integrity rests upon assumptions and proofs independent of application. Rather, it is how and why they are used that make the crucial difference. This conflict of means and ends in education is analogous to many troublesome aspects of modern society and world concerns. Heretofore, professional education has not been as involved in the debates of recent years over the universal feasibility and applicability of empirical approaches to knowledge. Somehow, those concerned with schools did not see how their scientific endeavors related to the controversies of means and ends that centered around dissidents such as C. Wright Mills. Perhaps a partial explanation is that professional education has lagged far behind other fields in adopting rational approaches, so that educational leaders have had cause to bemoan more the lack of scientific applications in schools than the over-use of them.

Standardized norms, statistical analyses, experimental designs, behavioral objectives, etc., have now become routinized in educational research and development. To many, such aspects of the scientific movement in education have become so prominent and ingrained that it seems heretical to probe their omnipotence, their proper status and function. Yet that kind of arrogance alone may indicate sufficient reason to do so; for many people, educational R & D has become almost synonymous with raw quantitative methods. The general usefulness of such approaches to enhance the quality of decision-making and the search for competing alternative procedures deserve close examination, since the influence of a dominant frame of reference upon the nation's educational enterprise can be inestimably great.

Most educational researchers and decision-makers, not to mention the typical educator, will feel adequate if asked to provide an in-depth rationale for their operational assumptions and procedures that is intellectually comprehensible and consistent in terms of the total and significant purposes of schools. However, the simplex retort that present approaches solve issues objectively and without verbal ambiguity does not square with the facts. Rational processes alone are not as successful in providing certainty and overcoming equivocality as many had believed. Educational issues, such as performance contracting and genetic heritability, in recent times, indicate that results from the empirical paradigm do not foreclose debate and indecision. Other points of contention and perspectives arise as much among empirical workers as from other approaches to knowledge and decision-making.

Significant federal support of educational R & D, starting in 1954, when Congress passed the Cooperative Research Act, is largely responsible for the recent advances in empirical work in education. Such funding demands the extension of organizational structures and the posture of proposing specific objectives, rational systematic methods, and the accounting of results. With a large input from federal sources, about $200 million is spent for educational R & D today. The amount is minuscule compared to nearly $70 billion in annual school expenditures and about $7.6 billion spent each year for defense R & D since 1969 and the $6 billion the Space Program consumed in 1966 alone, but it is great indeed compared to past support. The long-awaited National Institute of Education, which is modelled on the National Science Foundation and the National Institutes of Health, is now a reality. Since it will have a powerful long-range effect upon America's educational system, it will require careful attention as to perspective and, hopefully, will involve maximum opportunity for dialogue.

Comparing the progress of educational studies and the number of those involved in them before 1954 and today, we can only say that the difference is revolutionary. Besides having greater financial support, researchers benefit too from massive technical advances in processing and analyzing data and organizational structures in which they are the primary figures. Research and management skills and techniques in education are rapidly maturing, and the technical competence of those earning doctorates in education is more seriously developed than before. Without a doubt, educational research and development will continue to proliferate and improve for some time. It seems imperative that we conscientiously examine our modern procedures to see how well they relate to the basic purposes of education and values of society.

This symposium, therefore, will examine the area of management systems approaches, a key and representative feature of the rational frame, and assess its impact upon schools. Because the issue involves many ramifications and possible points of view, I gathered a highly competent and diverse group of scholars to thrash it out. A series of reactions to management systems approaches by group members and the opportunity to respond to each other seemed far better than attempting a solitary review and statement.

I must confess that the topic developed, for me, over a number of years, during which I attempted to conduct educational research and satisfy various dissonant viewpoints. A book on performance contracting that Dr. Robert E. Clasen of the *Journal of Educational Research* asked me to review last summer provided the necessary spur to develop a response. Many persons influenced this concern one way or the other, some of whom I do not know beyond their writings; but I will acknowledge Professor W.H. Cowley of Stanford University as being the first scholar to call my attention to the issue of contrasting research perspectives and values. He has continued to provide encouragement and helpful ideas over the years. A decade has passed since he suggested that I read *The Education of Henry Adams*, in which Adams' profound concern with modern science and technology, as epitomized by the electrical dynamo at the Great Exposition of 1900 in Chicago, impressed me very much.

The level and spirit of intellectual discourse that the other symposium participants have provided confirm my sense of good fortune in their willingness to participate. We came together as a symposium before a large and perceptive crowd at the 1972 American Educational Research Association meeting in Chicago, and have greatly extended our papers since that encouraging session to what is offered in this volume. I thank Dr. Wilson B. Thiede, publisher of the *Journal of Educational Research*, for permitting use of the first three papers.

Albert H. Yee

CONTENTS

perspectives on management systems approaches in education

1

The Adequacy of Systems Management Procedures in Education and Alternatives

Michael W. Apple

A few years ago, a well-known curriculum worker began his arguments for behavioral objectives—one of the precursors and usually a basic tenet of "systems management procedures" in education—with some rather interesting comments. Even though pointing to the necessity of dialogue for examining the respective worths of different positions on the controversial subject of designing educational activities in terms of "measurable learner behaviors," Popham had a few remarks to say that are quite pertinent to this paper.

Within the last few years a rather intense debate has developed in the field of curriculum and instruction regarding the merits of stating instructional objectives in terms of measurable learner behaviors. Because I am thoroughly committed, both rationally and viscerally, to the proposition that instructional goals should be stated behaviorally, I view this debate with some ambivalence. On the one hand, it is probably desirable to have a dialogue of this sort among specialists in our field. We get to know each other better—between attacks. We test the respective worths of opposing positions. We can have hopefully stimulating symposia such as this one. Yet as a partisan in the controversy, I would prefer unanimous support of the position to which I subscribe. You see, the other people are wrong. Adhering to a philosophic tenet that error is evil, I hate to see my friends wallowing in sin.

He then goes on to say:

Moreover, their particular form of sin is more dangerous than some of the time-honored perversions of civilized societies. For example, it will probably harm more people than the most exotic forms of pornography. I believe that those who discourage educators from precisely explicating their instructional objectives are often permitting, if not promoting, the same kind of unclear thinking that has led in part to the generally abysmal quality of instruction in this country.[1]

Now, I find this quote rather interesting. First, it documents the intellectual state of the curriculum field. While many of Schwab's specific criticisms of the curriculum field are tautologous, I tend to agree with his suggestion that the imminent death of a discipline is seen in its increasing use of *ad hominem* arguments[2] such as the one we have just quoted. Secondly, and of more important concern, the set of assumptions mirrored in the statement just quoted provides the ideological foundation for systems management in education. These assumptions are concerned with the tacit advocacy of a view negating the importance of intellectual conflict, a rather limited perspective on scientific endeavor, an inability to deal with ambiguity, and finally an outmoded separation of moral and technical questions. The increasing use of systems terminology in education rests on this set of beliefs—which, when examined, is often unrealistic, and socially and politically conservative.

At the outset, let me make certain of my perspectives clear. In my mind, schooling cannot be considered apart from the other economic and social institutions of a collectivity. It is intimately involved with and mirrors the dominant institutions of a society. Our thought about schooling and curriculum design is also fundamentally linked to the structure of the social order in which we exist.[3] While I would like to avoid a vulgar Marxist interpretation of consciousness, I would take the position that the basic framework of most curriculum rationality is generally supportive and accepting of the *existing* economic, political, and intellectual framework that apportions opportunity in American society. I do not ask the reader to share my perceptions that this framework tends toward the sublimation of basic human sentiment and the repression of a large portion of people within it. What I do ask is that the perceptions not be dismissed offhand, and that curriculists cease to act on tacit assumptions which prevent them from focusing upon the definite ideological and epistemological commitments they possess. Part of the task of curriculum scholarship is to bring to a level of awareness the latent dysfunctions of our work, for values continually work through us and are sedimented within the very mind set we apply to our problems. It may very well be the case that the often inhuman and problematic activities and consequences of schooling will not be fundamentally altered until we cease searching for simple solutions to our problems. Part of the answer, but only part, is to illuminate our political and conceptual orientations. It is possible that the two are considerably interwoven.

I would like to point to tendencies in systems management procedures that often have some interesting things to say about the curriculum field's social commitments. For example, I shall consider systems language as conservative social rhetoric and shall look behind it to portray its incorrect view of science. First, let us look at systems thought as a general intellectual framework in education. Let me state, however, that the points to be made here apply to the educational uses of systems logic and not necessarily to systems thought *per se* (though this latter point does remain moot).

Systems and Technical Control

Usually, one engages in systems approaches to obtain a more exact and "scientific" analysis. However, the view of scientific activity underpinning the use of systems strategies in education and curriculum design is based less upon an accurate view of scientific processes than it is upon an after-the-fact examination of scientific products. A distinction that is helpful here is one between the *logic-in-use* of a science and its *reconstructed* logic.[4] The former connotes what scientists actually do; and that is *not* necessarily the linear progression of stating goals absolutely clearly, of hypothesis testing and verification or falsification through statistical or other analyses, and so forth. The latter connotes what observers, philosophers of science, and others say that the *logic* of scientific inquiry looks like. There has been an exceptionally long history in educational thought, from Snedden up to the present, of borrowing a reconstructed logic of scientific activity and expecting it to be sufficient for treating the complex problem of curriculum design, to say nothing of curriculum "research."

This has usually taken the form of the development of procedures to guarantee certainty and to rationalize and make explicit as many aspects of peoples' activity as possible, be it the researcher, the educational decision-maker, or the student. Huebner has described this approach as "technological" in that it seeks to use strict forms of means-ends or process-product reasoning and is primarily interested in efficiency, thus tending to exclude other modes of valuing.[5] Examples include the early work of Bobbitt on activity analysis, which seemed to crystallize the basic paradigm of the field of curriculum, and the later emphasis on behavioral objectives. Each of these has sought to specify the operational boundaries of institutional interaction and has been motivated by a need for closure and, especially, surety. The behavioral objectives movement, for instance, in both its weak and strong senses, has sought to reduce student action to specifiable forms of overt behavior so that the educator can have certitude of outcome. While the need for certainty is understandable, given the large sums of money spent on education, its superficiality is disturbing. The behavioral orientation itself (as well as many constitutive aspects of systems management approaches) has been effectively dealt with by such early treatments as Ryle's analysis of knowing in its dispositional vs. achievement senses, by Polanyi's exploration of forms of tacit knowing, and in Hannah Arendt's masterful examination of how the need for certainty often precludes the creation of personal meaning and effectively weakens the base of political action.[6] These analytic concerns aside, however, the perspective on systems as enabling a more "scientific" approach to educational problems requires further investigation.

Unlike the unceasing quest for surety among educators, scientific activity has been less characterized by a preference for certainty, for the slow and steady accumulation of technical data, than we have supposed. What most members of the scientific community would label "good science" is a process that is constituted upon the leap of faith, an aesthetic sensitivity, a personal commitment, and—of great importance—an ability to accept ambiguity and uncertainty.[7] Without such qualities, ones which maintain the scientific enterprise as an essentially human and changing artifact, science becomes mere technology. The view of science that is used to give legitimacy to a good deal of curriculum thought, especially that of systems approaches, is more reminiscent of a nineteenth century brand of positivism than it is of current scientific and philosophical discourse. While the trend toward naive reductionism, for example, in approaching human action was stemmed in philosophy by 1930 or so,[8] much of curriculum rationality today, as we shall see, has progressed no further.

The problem of drawing upon a reconstructed logic is further compounded by our belief in the inherent neutrality of systems management. There seems to be a tacit assumption that systems management procedures are merely "scientific" techniques; they are interest-free and can be applied to "engineer" nearly any problem one faces. A searching analysis discloses some provocative questions about this assumption, however. To be accurate, systems management procedures are not interest-free. Their own constitutive interest lies primarily in, and has the social consequence of, effecting and maintaining *technical control* and *certainty*.[9]

Like the reconstructed logic of the strict sciences, systems management is aimed, fundamentally and unalterably, at the regularities of human behavior, the language of "individual differences" to the contrary. It is, hence, essentially manipulative. The manipulative perspective is inherent in the quest for certainty. In fact it is difficult to envision how an unflinching requirement for exactitude in goals and behavioral specifications can be less than manipulative, given the propensities of man to exist in a dialectical relationship with his social reality—that is, to make meaning his own and go beyond the framework and texture of socially sedimented meanings and institutions.[10] It is here that we find a primary example of the conservative orientation so deeply embedded in "technological" models of educational thought.

A similar point is made by Sennett in his discussion of the tendency of city planners to create systems whose ideal is that nothing "be out of control," for institutional life "to be manipulated on so tight a rein [that] all manner of diverse activities must be ruled by the lowest common denominator."[11] He summarizes his analysis of the propensity of systems planners to use technological and production models thus:

> Their impulse has been to give way to that tendency . . . of men to control unknown threats by eliminating the possibility of experiencing surprise. By controlling the frame of what is available for social interaction, the subsequent path of social action is tamed. Social history is replaced by the passive "product" of social planning. Buried in this hunger for preplanning along machine-like lines is the desire to avoid pain, to create a

transcendent order of living that is immune to the
variety, and so the inevitable conflict, between
men.[12]

The philosophical naivety and the strikingly deterministic aspect of systems management as it is applied in
education is perhaps most evident in the dictum that requires
of those building instructional systems, for instance, to
"formulate specific learning objectives, clearly stating whatever the learner is expected to be able to *do, know,* and *feel*
as an outcome of his learning experiences."[13] Even a surface
examination of the psychological and especially the philosophical analyses of the nature of dispositions, attainments,
and propensities, and how these are "taught" and linked with
other types of "knowledge," shows the lack of any significant amount of thought being given to how human beings do,
in fact, operate in real life.[14] Furthermore, the reductive
mentality, one in which the components of cognition are
divorced from "feeling" and can be behaviorally specified,
fundamentally misconstrues the nature of human action.[15]
The very idea that educators should specify *all* or even the
primary aspects of a person's action substitutes the slogan of
manipulation for the awe-ful task of making moral choices.

It should be made clear that curriculum design, the
creating of educative environments in which students are to
dwell, is inherently a political and moral process. It involves
competing ideological, political, and intensely personal conceptions of valuable educational activity. Furthermore, one
of its primary components is the fact of influencing other
people—namely students. Our common-sense thought in
education, however, tends to move in a direction quite the
opposite from moral and political considerations. Instead,

spheres of decision-making are perceived as *technical problems* that only necessitate instrumental strategies and information produced by technical experts,[16] hence effectively removing the decisions from the realm of political and ethical debate. In other words, even though rationales such as systems procedures cloak themselves in the language of "being realistic," there is a strong tendency in their use to flatten reality, to define the complex valuative issues out of existence by using a form of thought that is amenable only to technical competence. In essence, the employment of systems procedures qua formula tends to obscure for the educator the fact that he is making profound ethical decisions about a group of other human beings.

Now, the real issue is not that systems techniques yield information and feedback that may be used *by* systems of social control. They themselves *are* systems of control.[17] What is of equal importance is the fact that the belief system underlying them and a major portion of the curriculum field stems from and functions as a technocratic ideology which often can serve to legitimate the existing distribution of power and privilege in our society.[18] The very language used by a number of proponents of systems management in education conveys their assumptions. While change is viewed as important, it is usually dealt with by such notions as system *adjustment*.[19] The basis of the system itself remains unquestioned. The use of systems procedures assumes as its taken-for-granted foundation that the institutions of schooling are fundamentally sound. That is, while "the quality of instruction" is often poor, the same general pattern of human interaction is sufficient for education, if the institution can be "tuned up," so to speak. The problems of schooling are to be solved by modest inputs of centralized administration, along with expert services, research, and advice. The lack of quality in education is viewed in terms of only a lack of technical sophistication and can be effectively solved through engineering.[20] The increasing disaffection with much of the obligatory meaning structure of schooling by students belies this perception.

Like the Tyler rationale before it, systems management assumes that the effectiveness of a system can be evaluated by "how closely the output of the system satisfies the purpose for which it exists."[21] However, in the quest for orderliness, the political process by which often competing visions of purposes deal with each other and come to some sort of understanding is virtually ignored. Again, like Tyler, one—the manager of an institution perhaps—"engineers" in an unreal world. An understanding of the difficult ethical, ideological, and even aesthetic problems, of who decides what and what these purposes should be, that exist in the real world of education is advanced no further.

Systems design itself is an analytic procedure in its own right, with its own history and, usually, its own modes of self-correction when kept *within* its tradition. However, the educational orientation labeled "systems design" does not approach this sophistication; nor does it borrow more than a veneer of terminology, which is used to cover the dominant metaphor curriculists have used to look at schooling for over fifty years. This metaphor, or model, pictures the school as a factory, and traces its roots back to the beginnings of curriculum as a field of study, especially to the work of Bobbitt and Charters.[22] In systems analysis in the field of computer design, inputs and outputs are *information;* in systems procedures in education, they are often children. The school is the processing plant and the "educated man" is the "product."[23] Given the fact that a field's language and metaphoric constructs often determine its mode of operation, the use of the language of child-qua-product is apt to preserve and enhance the already strikingly manipulative ethos of schooling. The ethos is also fostered by the relative lack of insight educators have into the domain of systems thought itself.

One is hard pressed to find more than occasional references in the literature on systems management procedures in the curriculum field, for example, to the most creative systems theorists. The structuralism of a Von Bertalanffy is nearly absent, as is the subtlety of the way he attempts to grapple with problems. While one does find a few references to him, it is quite obvious that the fundamental notions about systems procedures are not drawn from this school of thought. Rather, one sees a model that is actually taken from such fields as weapons technology and industry.[24] What is not found is of considerable moment, given our attempt to be "scientific." What is found, though, is the encasing of the school-as-factory model in a layer of slogans to give the field intellectual and economic legitimacy and a sense of neutrality. Systems design as a field of scientific study has within itself self-correcting mechanisms. The continual criticism of research and thought, and the intellectual conflict within the systems field among members of varying persuasions, provide a context for keeping it vital. Educators have borrowed only the language, often only the surface language (what I have called the reconstructed logic), and have, hence, pulled the terminology out of its self-correcting context. Thus, they have little insight into the continuing critical dialogue in the field of systems design that enables it to remain potent. We have yet to learn the dangers of appropriating models from disparate fields and applying them to education. All too frequently, the models are quickly outmoded, are intellectually inaccurate representations of those developed in the lending field,[25] and provide little in the way of the conceptual resources needed to grapple with the complex problem of designing environments which mediate between a student's search for personal meaning and a society's need to preserve its socially sedimented fabric of institutions and knowledge.

Systems analysis began *not* as a management technique but as a mode by which the complex nature of problems could be illuminated. It sought to show how components of a field were interrelated and acted upon one another. Systems analysis was a mode of thought that sought to enhance our comprehension of change and stability—subsystem A is related in X fashion to subsystem B which in turn is related in Y fashion to subsystem C. The combination created a different relationship, Z. Any alteration of C, therefore, would have profound repercussions in A and B, and in all the linkages between them. Systems thought, then, was a model for understanding, not necessarily for control. However, many curriculists seem to be employing it to manage their problems without first understanding the complexity of the relationships themselves. This is one of the points in which Schwab is correct. Only when we begin to see the intricate nature of the relationships among the aspects of the educational environment[26] can we begin to act as more than technicians. As a model for disclosing possibilities, not as a picture of what should be, systems analysis has its place. As a management structure for making institutional meanings obligatory, it is less than neutral, to say the least.

While the advocates of systems procedures seek to

enhance the scientific status of their work, the systems thought they have borrowed is not from the scientific branch of systems logic, as I have pointed out. Rather, they have chosen to appropriate the models of operation of the business community.[27] This is not new by any means, of course.[28] While it would be unfair to point out that such "successful" concerns as Lockheed are the major proponents of systems procedures for large-scale endeavors, it would not be inaccurate to point out that the business and economic substructure of the United States continues to generate avenues that provide extremely limited opportunities for nearly *one-sixth* of the total population. One has to wonder if their models are indeed appropriate for dealing with students.

There are other issues that could be raised about the idea that systems procedures are "scientific" and are neutral techniques for establishing better educational practices. As I have noted, it is one of the basic assumptions that must be examined rather closely. I would like to delve a bit further and raise a few questions about its possible latent conservatism. One question concerns itself with systems language as a social rhetoric; the other concerns a constitutive aspect of systems procedures as they are applied today in education— namely, the specification of precise instructional and usually behavioral objectives as tacitly preserving in an unquestioning manner the dominant modes of institutional interaction in an industrial economy. I will then examine how the penchant for order in curriculum today serves a similar function. Let us first examine the issue of systems as a language.

Systems Procedures as Rhetoric
The Wittgensteinian principle that the meaning of

language depends on its use is quite appropriate for analyzing systems language as it is applied in curriculum discourse. Systems language performs a rhetorical and political function. Without an understanding of this, we miss a major point. One of its primary, if latent, uses is to convince others of the sophisticated state of education. If a field can convince funding agencies, government, or the populace in general that scientific procedures are being employed, whether or not they are in fact helpful, then the probability of increased monetary and political support is heightened. Given the high esteem in which science is held in industrial nations, this is important. (Unfortunately, it is not science *per se* that is seen positively; rather it is technology and its concrete applicability.) Couching a field's problems in systems terminology evokes tacit meanings from a general audience, meanings that are supportive of a quasi-scientific belief system. More importantly, since educational experimentation almost always follows funding, systems language has as a primary function the political task of generating money from the federal government. Hence we can expect the "little science, big science" controversy that still rages in the physical sciences to rear its head in education as well.[29] Given the alternative pressure for decentralization, the question of funding and control *cannot* be ignored. Systems management procedures have a tendency toward centralization, even without the issue of funding and rhetoric. In order to be most effective, as many variables as possible—interpersonal, economic, etc.—must be brought under and controlled by the system itself. Order and consensus become strikingly important; conflict and disorder are perceived as antithetical to the smooth functioning of the system. The fact that conflict and disorder are extraordinarily important to prevent the reification of institutional patterns of interaction is, thus, ignored.[30]

The *content* of systems procedures is empty. Systems thought is a formal set, or methodology, if you will, that can be applied to educational problems. That is, its conceptual emptiness enables its application in a supposedly "neutral" manner to a range of problems requiring the precise formulation of goals, procedures, and feedback devices. Since systems methodology communicates this sense of neutrality, it is ideally suited to foster consensus around it.[31] This process of consensus formation, and the avoidance of conflict, enables the interests of the administrative managers of institutions to direct the questions one asks about schooling.

This evocation of tacit meanings is crucial in examining systems management thought. Not only are supportive feelings generated, but political quiescence is also enhanced. For example, it may be the case that the common school and the ideological underpinnings that support it have *never* served to educate, say, racial minorities in the United States.[32] It may also be the case that schools have served basically to apportion and distribute opportunities that are consistently unequal in terms of economic class. What the employment of sophisticated "scientific" rationales can do by evoking supportive sentiment, then, is to prevent a portion of the population from seeing that schools as they exist by and large simply cannot meet the needs of minority and other populations. The very institutional status of schools is caught up in a variety of other institutional forms—economic, for instance—that enhance the existing political and economic structures.

This quiescence is brought about in a two-pronged

fashion and is aimed at two publics. First, systems management language is pronounced to critics of ongoing educational activity—again, let us use the example of minority groups—and is often coupled with the notion of "accountability," thereby giving them the feeling that something is in fact being done.[33] After all, it does sound concise and straightforward. But this is not the essential prong. After all, ghetto dwellers, for example, may not be as enamored of technical terminology and have little political power, nor do they influence economic resources and funding as much as the second set of groups to which this language is aimed. The primary audience includes the members of the general population and industry[34] whose sentiments often resonate strongly to technical expertise and industrial logic. Even when the members of minority groups may have determined over a period of time that school life has been made no less overtly repressive, as has been the case so often, the other more powerful public, due to the depth of the taken-for-granted acceptance of the benefits of technical rationality and technical expertise in solving human problems, will probably remain generally supportive.

To be accurate, one other public should be mentioned. These are the users of systems language themselves. Much of the history of curriculum discourse over the last fifty years or so has been indicative of a need on the part of curriculum workers to have their field become more like a science. I will not dwell upon the possibility of psychoanalyzing this need for prestige. However, a latent function of systems approaches is, no doubt, that it psychologically confirms curriculum workers' ties to a sought-after reference group—here the scientific community, and, as we have noted and shall reiterate, a misperceived scientific community at that.

It should be made clear, then, that systems approaches are not essentially neutral, nor are they only performing a "scientific" function. By tending to cause its users and the other publics involved to ignore certain possible fundamental problems with schools as institutions, systems management also acts to generate and channel political sentiments supportive of the existing modes of access to knowledge and power.[35]

Besides performing these political functions associated with funding and "affective" support, the rhetorical function of system terminology and of technical methodologies tends to uphold the dominance of existing institutions in another way. Dealing with a type of systems thought in sociology, Gouldner makes the provocative statement that aside from serving "to defocalize the ideological dimensions of decision-making, diverting attention from differences in ultimate values and from the more remote consequences of the social policies to which its research is harnessed," supposedly value-free technical perspectives provide the solution to an elite group of managers' problems,[36] not the complex and fundamental valuative issues that we face in, say, education concerning the proper ways to educate children, or the issues of education vs. training, and freedom and authority. Gouldner summarizes this quite well by saying:

> As . . . funding becomes increasingly available, the emphasis on rigorous methodologies assumes a special rhetorical function. It serves to provide a framework for resolving limited differences among the managers of organizations and institutions, who have little conflict over basic values or social mappings, by lending the sanction of science to

limited policy choices concerning ways and means. At the same time, its cognitive emphasis serves to defocalize the conflict of values that remain involved in political differences, and to focus contention on questions of fact, implying that the value conflict may be resolved apart from politics and without political conflict. Positivism [and perspectives such as systems management stemming partly from it, I would add] thus continue to serve as ways of avoiding conflicts about mapping. Yet despite this seemingly neutral, non-partisan character, [these perspectives'] social impact is not random or neutral in regard to competing social mappings; because of [their] emphasis on the problem of social order, because of the social origins, education and character of [their] own personnel, and because of the dependencies generated by [their] funding requirements, [they] persistently tend to support the status quo.[37]

Gouldner's argument is rather interesting and is one we all should reflect upon. Is systems management "merely" a mode by which an institutional and managerial elite avoids conflict over *basic* values and educational visions? By making choices about limited options within the framework of existing modes of interaction, are questions about the basis of the structure itself precluded? How, for instance, would systems management procedures deal with the clash of two competing ideologies about schooling where goals cannot be easily defined? These questions require much closer scrutiny if educational institutions are to be responsive to their varied publics.

I have made the point throughout this paper so far that the consciousness of curriculum workers themselves as well as other educators can be seen as latently political and often somewhat conservative. That is, they use forms of thought that at least partially stem from and can tacitly act to maintain the existing social and economic substructure and distribution of power in an industrial society such as our own. Systems management procedures offer an intriguing example of this problem. I shall give one more example.

A significant part of the framework of systems management is concerned with and is based upon the precise formulation of goals, on a micro-system level, usually with the specification of behavioral goals. That is, a student's behavior is preselected *before* he engages in educational activity, and this behavior is used as the end-product of the system so that feedback can be gained. Ultimately this will feed upwards on a macro-system level for the management of large systems. Let us examine this. The process/product style of reasoning employed here, one that is most evident in the call for behavioral objectives, is quite functional to a society that requires a large proportion of its workers to engage in often boring assembly-line labor or in personally unimportant white-collar work. By learning how to work for others' preordained goals, using others' preselected behaviors, students also learn to function in an increasingly bureaucratized society in which the adult roles one is to play are already sedimented into the social fabric. Each role has its own brand of thinking *already* built into it,[38] and students will feel comfortable playing these often relatively alienating roles only insofar as they have been taught that this is the proper mode of existing. Curriculists, by internalizing and using an orientation that lends itself to such preordination, cannot help but contribute to the maintenance of a political and economic order that creates and maintains these roles and the meaning already distributed within them.[39] This problem is intricately involved with the perspective on disorder that most educators share.

Systems, Science, and Consensus

The view on order and conflict mirrored in a good deal of the way systems approaches are employed in education is striking. It is indicative of a constitutive rule of activity that causes most of us to see order as positive and conflict as negative.[40] Order becomes a psychological necessity. This is rather important. As I mentioned before, systems approaches attempt to bring about a technical solution to political and value problems. There is nothing odd about this occurrence. Most advanced industrial societies seem to transform their ethical, political, and aesthetic questions, for instance, into engineering problems.[41] Profound conflict between opposing ideological and moral positions are translated into puzzles to be solved by technical expertise. Now, when questioned about the tendency to eliminate conflict, or redefine it, and search for consensus, proponents of systems management procedures in education could and do, in fact, take the position that they are merely trying to be scientific about their problems. This is where a basic difficulty lies. The perspective they have of science is notably inaccurate in ways other than those to which we referred earlier in our discussion.

In the quote on precise instructional objectives at the beginning of this paper, we saw a perspective that legitimated intellectual consensus, one that asked for total agreement on the "paradigm" to be used in curriculum thought so that we could be more scientific. In fact, those who looked askance at the accepted paradigm were, in effect, labelled as deviants. Such universe-maintaining verbal activity is not wrong in itself nor is it unusual.[42] To link scientific rationality with consensus, however, is to do a disservice to science and shows a profound misunderstanding of the history of the scientific disciplines.

The history of science and the growth of individual disciplines has *not* proceeded by consensus. In fact, most important progress in these fields has been occasioned by intense conflict, both intellectual and interpersonal, and by conceptual revolution.[43] It is primarily by such conflict that significant advancement is made, not primarily by the accumulation of factual data based on the solving of puzzles generated by a paradigm all must share. The very normative structure of scientific communities tends toward skepticism and not necessarily toward intellectual consensus.[44] The call for consensus, thus, is not a call for science.

One thing that the quote does make clear, however, is the intense personal commitment that accepted modes of thought generate. This is probably true in any field. It does put somewhat of a damper on our traditional concept of neutrality, though. Accepted thought becomes a psychological and valuative commitment, a norm of behavior. Scientists are intensely and personally committed,[45] and this is one of the primary sources of conflict within disciplines. Hence, to call for consensus is to call for a *lack* of commitment and is to ignore the crucial value of the uncertain and of conceptual conflict in a field's progress. The covert request for a lack of commitment is of considerable moment. Systems management terminology, as was mentioned, tends to impose technical solutions on moral dilemmas—what is the proper way to influence another human being, for instance. If moral commitments are less firm, the task of flattening reality is made that much easier.

The Search for Alternatives

There are ways of dealing with some of the possible difficulties associated with the use of systems management procedures in education. First, educators must engage in continuous and in-depth analysis of other forms of systems thought. The lenses of open systems and biological systems could provide excellent disclosure models for further examination. Second, they can immerse themselves in the issues and controversies *within* the systems field so that they are aware of the concrete theoretic and practical difficulties facing systems analysis as a field. In this way, educators may prevent a further recapitulation of their history of borrowing knowledge that is taken out of its self-correcting context and, hence, is often surface or one-sided. While the use of systems approaches has an obvious immediate plausibility, we do not do justice to the intellectual complexity associated with systems thought itself or to the intricate nature of instructional relationships in education (which systems approaches can at least partially illuminate) if we base our analyses upon conceptions of systems that may be given only a weak warrant within the larger systems community. There are alternatives within systems discourse that educators have yet to explore in a rigorous fashion.

This rigorous exploration will not eliminate all of the difficulties, however, for there are a number of other questions one could raise concerning systems management procedures. Perhaps one of the more crucial ones centers around the very real possibility of increasing bureaucratization through the total rationalization of education. This is not to raise the spectre of a bureaucratic machine overrunning human concerns. Rather, it asks us to be realistic, if not tragic. Anyone familiar with the growth of urban schools knows that the history of rationalizing and centralizing decision-making, no matter what the humane sentiments behind it, has nearly invariably led to institutional crystallization and reification.[46] The fact that we are not familiar with our own history concerning "reforms" of this nature merely documents the simplicity with which we approach our problems.

There are no easy alternatives to a management and control ideology. One could easily show the epistemological and psychological problems associated with behavioral objectives,[47] for instance; or one could document the fact that the Tyler rationale in curriculum is little more than an administrative document that does not adequately deal with the concrete reality of schools. Yet this type of activity treats such behavioristic rationales as if they were logically founded and scientifically arguable. It may very well be that they are not. As I have tried to show, what they do seem to be are expressions of a dominant industrialized consciousness that seeks certainty above all else. That is, they are social and ideological configurations stemming from and mirroring a set of basic rules of thought that are part of the taken-for-granted reality of curriculum workers and other educators. The reality inclines us to search for relatively easy ways to eliminate the human dilemmas (even mysteries) of dealing with diversity and alternative conceptions of valued activity.

To ask, then, for *a* substitute or *one* alternative to systems management procedures is to confirm the assumption that utterly complex problems can be resolved easily within the accepted framework, and without the ambiguous and awe-ful necessity of engaging in the crucial task of challenging or at least illuminating the framework itself. The task is not to find the *one* acceptable alternative that will enable us "merely" to control our schools better. Rather, it is to begin to disclose the problems associated with our common-sense views of schooling and to begin to open up and explore avenues that seem fruitful and may enable us to see the complexity rather than define it out of existence.

Systems metaphors as *models of understanding* may prove helpful here. But there are prior questions with which we need to grapple. We must learn (perhaps "relearn" is more accurate[48]) how to engage in serious ethical and political debate. In this, educators can be guided by the work in philosophical analysis dealing with modes of moral reasoning and valuative argumentation. Such investigations as Rawls' recent attempt at explicating warranted moral stands[49] takes on an increasing importance given the intense controversy surrounding schools today.

Alternative visions of institutional alignments are also critical to prevent the reification of the present into the future. The field lacks the disciplined aesthetic sense and imagination to envision possibilities of disparate educative environments. It is quite possible that the perceived need for operationally pre-specified outcomes mitigates against the development of such imagination.[50]

Finally, a significant part of curriculum as a field must be devoted to the responsibility of becoming a critical science. Its primary function is to be emancipatory in that it critically reflects upon the field's dominant interest in keeping most, if not all, aspects of human behavior in educational institutions under technical control.[51] Such a responsibility is rooted in seeking out and illuminating the ideological and epistemological presuppositions of curriculum thought. It seeks to make curriculum workers more self-aware. Only when this dialectic of critical awareness is begun can curriculists truthfully state that they are concerned with education and not training. It is then that we may begin to explore in a rigorous fashion the complex problems of designing and valuing educational environments[52] in a variety of ways.

Notes

1. W. James Popham, "Probing the validity of arguments against behavioral goals," reprinted in Robert J. Kibler *et al.*, *Behavioral objectives and instruction* (Boston: Allyn and Bacon, 1970), pp. 115-116.
2. Joseph J. Schwab, *The practical: A language for curriculum* (Washington, D.C.: National Education Association, 1970), p. 18.
3. Cf. the excellent analysis of the relationship between knowledge and institutions in Peter L. Berger and Thomas Luckmann, *The social-construction of reality* (N.Y.: Doubleday Anchor Books, 1966).
4. Abraham Kaplan, *The conduct of inquiry* (San Francisco: Chandler, 1964), pp. 3-11.
5. Dwayne Huebner, "Curricular language and classroom meanings," *Language and meaning*, James B. Macdonald and Robert R. Leeper, editors (Washington, D.C.: Association for Supervision and Curriculum Development, 1966), pp. 8-26.
6. Cf. Gilbert Ryle, *The concept of mind* (N.Y.: Barnes and Noble, 1949), Michael Polanyi, *The tacit dimension* (N.Y.: Doubleday Anchor Books, 1966), and Hannah

Arendt, *The human condition* (N.Y.: Doubleday Anchor Books, 1958).

7. See, for example, the discussion of wave vs. particle theories of light in Thomas S. Kuhn, *The structure of scientific revolutions* (Chicago: University of Chicago Press, 1970). See also Imre Lakatos and Alan Musgrave, eds., *Criticism and the growth of knowledge* (Cambridge: Cambridge University Press, 1970) and Michael Polanyi, *Personal Knowledge* (N.Y.: Harper Torchbooks, 1964).

8. J.O. Urmson, *Philosophical analysis* (London: Oxford University Press, 1956), p. 146.

9. Trent Schroyer, "Toward a critical theory for advanced industrial society," *Recent sociology 2*, Hans Peter Dreitzel, editor (N.Y.: Macmillan, 1970), p. 215; and Jurgen Habermas, "Knowledge and interest," *Sociological theory and philosophical analysis*, Dorothy Emmet and Alastair MacIntyre, editors (N.Y.: Macmillan, 1970), pp. 36-54.

10. Peter L. Berger and Thomas Luckmann, *op. cit.*, p. 129.

11. Richard Sennett, *The uses of disorder* (N.Y.: Vintage Books, 1970), p. 94.

12. *Ibid.*, p. 96.

13. Bela H. Banathy, *Instructional systems* (Palo Alto, California: Fearon, 1968), p. 22. My stress.

14. Cf. Donald Arnstine, *Philosophy of education: Learning and schooling* (N.Y.: Harper and Row, 1967) and Stuart Hampshire, *Thought and action* (N.Y.: The Viking Press, 1959).

15. This naive separation and the destructive aspects of behavioral specification can often best be seen in discussions of scientific thought, especially that of Michael Polanyi, *op. cit.*; Susanne Langer's analysis of "mind" in *Philosophy in a new key* (N.Y.: Mentor,

1951) is also quite helpful here.
16. Schroyer, *op. cit.*, p. 212.
17. Alvin W. Gouldner, *The coming crisis of western sociology* (N.Y.: Basic Books, 1970), p. 50.
18. Schroyer, *op. cit.*, p. 210.
19. Banathy, *op. cit.*, p. 10.
20. Gouldner, *op. cit.*, p. 161.
21. Banathy, *op. cit.*, p. 13.
22. Herbert M. Kliebard, "Bureaucracy and curriculum theory," *Freedom, bureaucracy, and schooling*, Vernon Haubrich, editor (Washington, D.C.: Association for Supervision and Curriculum Development, 1971), pp. 74-93. This is not an unconscious linkage to the work of early theorists such as the sometimes quite problematic work of Bobbitt. See, for example, Robert Kibler *et al.*, *Behavioral objectives and instruction* (Boston: Allyn & Bacon, 1970), p. 105.
23. Banathy, *op. cit.*, p. 17.
24. *Ibid.*, p. 2.
25. Perhaps one of the more interesting examples of this is reflected in the work of Snedden. His appropriation of the worst of sociology served conservative ideological concerns. See Walter Drost, *David Snedden and education for social efficiency* (Madison: The University of Wisconsin Press, 1967). Yet another instance is our increasing use of learning theory. Not only has it told us little that is applicable to the complex day-to-day reality of educational life, but we have been persistently unaware of the problems learning theory itself has within its own scholarly community. The most complete analysis of the conceptual difficulties can be found in Charles Taylor, *The explanation of behavior* (N.Y.: The Humanities Press, 1964), and Maurice Merleau-Ponty, *The structure of behavior* (Boston: Beacon Press, 1963).

26. Schwab, *op. cit.*, pp. 33-35.
27. Bruce R. Joyce *et al.*, *Implementing systems models for teacher education* (Washington, D.C.: U.S. Department of Health, Education and Welfare, 1971).
28. See Raymond Callahan, *Education and the cult of efficiency* (Chicago: University of Chicago Press, 1962).
29. Cf. Derek J. de Solla Price, *Little science, big science* (N.Y.: Columbia University Press, 1963) and Warren O. Hagstrom, *The scientific community* (N.Y.: Basic Books, 1965).
30. Michael W. Apple, "The hidden curriculum and the nature of conflict," *Interchange*, 1971, *2*, 4, 27-40.
31. Gouldner, *op. cit.*, p. 445.
32. Colin Greer, "Immigrants, Negroes, and the public schools," *The Urban Review*, III (January, 1969), 9-12.
33. The use of the language of relevance by schoolmen to feed back to educational critics in the ghetto to bring about quiescence is extremely similar in this respect. Michael W. Apple, "Relevance—slogans and meanings," *The Educational Forum*, XXXV (May, 1971), 503-507.
34. Murray Edelman, *Politics as symbolic action* (Chicago: Markham, 1971).
35. Compare here to the discussion of systems theory in sociology as being a tacit theory of conservative politics as well in Gouldner, *op. cit.*
36. *Ibid.*, p. 105.
37. *Ibid.*
38. Erving Goffman, *The presentation of self in everyday life* (N.Y.: Doubleday Anchor, 1959).
39. Berger and Luckmann, *op. cit.*
40. Michael W. Apple, "The hidden curriculum and the nature of conflict," *op. cit.*
41. See, for instance, the provocative but often overdrawn and analytically troublesome examination in Jacques

Ellul, *The technological society* (N.Y.: Vintage, 1964).

42. Berger and Luckmann, *op. cit.,* p. 105.

43. Kuhn, *op. cit.* For a more in-depth discussion of the place of conflict in science, see Apple, "The hidden curriculum and the nature of conflict," *op. cit.*

44. Norman W. Storer, *The social system of science* (N.Y.: Holt, Rinehart and Winston, 1966), pp. 78-79.

45. Polanyi, *op. cit.*

46. Carl Kaestle, personal communication.

47. Michael W. Apple, "Behaviorism and conservatism," *Perspectives for reform in teacher education,* Bruce R. Joyce and Marsha Weil, editors (Englewood Cliffs, N.J.: Prentice Hall, 1972).

48. Arendt's, *op. cit.,* treatment of the forms of argumentation and political and personal action of the polis is helpful here.

49. John Rawls, *A theory of justice* (Cambridge: Harvard University Press, 1971).

50. See the interesting debate in *Interchange,* 1971, *2,* 1, on alternatives to existing modes of schooling. Nearly the entire issue is devoted to the topic. On the necessity of imaginative vision in education, see William Walsh, *The use of imagination* (N.Y.: Barnes and Noble, 1959).

51. Habermas, *op. cit.,* p. 45.

52. Two papers by Huebner are quite important in this regard. See Dwayne Huebner, "Curriculum as the accessibility of knowledge," a paper presented at the Curriculum Theory Study Group, Minneapolis, March 2, 1970, and "The tasks of the curricular theorist," a paper presented at the meeting of the Association for Supervision and Curriculum Development, Atlantic City, March, 1968.

2

Objectives-Based Management Strategies for Large Educational Systems

W. James Popham

There is an apparent defect in human nature which disinclines us to subject any enterprise to careful scrutiny until we sense it is in some way defective. Without debating whether this failing stems from original sin or is merely an acquired shortcoming, there is little doubt that we are currently witnessing the results of this tendency in the field of education.

American citizens in increasing numbers have become disenchanted with the quality of our educational system, and the magnitude of this disenchantment has now passed the critical point, so that rhetoric no longer satisfies, and corrective action is being demanded. The problem facing us now is easier to articulate than to answer, namely, "How should we go about promoting improvements in the educational enterprise?"

Systems Analysis Strategies

Some educators are turning to systems analysis methodology as a possible source for satisfactory answers to this perplexing question. In certain of these systems analysis proponents one senses an almost religious devotion to their methodology, a devotion in which the litany of input analysis, output analysis, and servoloop feedback must be chanted daily—or at least in every published article and speech.

For me, however, systems analysis approaches derive their merits not because they border on the occult but, rather, because they reflect a rational attempt to illuminate the arenas in which we must make educational decisions. If most people are left to their own devices when they must make decisions, they will usually find that erroneous perceptions of reality and unconcious biases render those decisions less than satisfactory. Surely there are many wise human beings who will reach enlightened decisions which all of us would applaud, but there are many others who do not operate as meritoriously. If the decisions affect only themselves, we are not all that upset if the wrong choice is made; after all, an individual pretty well has the right to make up his own life if he wishes. But in the field of education we see that imprudent decisions can penalize thousands of students; thus we cannot remain as sanguine regarding intuitively based decision-making. Therefore we find an increasing number of people, both educators and non-educators, advocating the use of more formal mechanisms for making decisions regarding large-scale educational enterprises. Customarily, these mechanisms have taken a form which more or less resembles a systems analysis approach.

The distinguishing feature of a systems analysis strategy is implied by its name. Clearly, there is an attempt to analyze a system of some sort, in this instance an educational system. But equally critical is the implication that this analysis will be a *systematic* one. Indeed, many people are enamored of systems analysis approaches for precisely that reason, i.e., they tend to reduce the capricious decision-making which is so characteristic of most human endeavors.

There is another dimension characteristically associated with systems analysis approaches which should be noticed, namely, a reliance on *evidence* of the system's effects. This orientation is in contrast to alternative approaches which, although systematic and analytic, are not essentially empirical methodologies. For instance, analytic philosophical approaches are generally not considered to be systems analysis strategies, even though they may epitomize rigorous analysis.

Large-Scale Educational Systems

This discussion will be restricted to the consideration of large-scale educational enterprises, such as a state school system or a large school district.

This does not suggest that the following observations are inappropriate for small systems such as a moderate-sized school district or even a single school. Yet, in general, the focus will be on the recommendations for systems of sufficient magnitude to warrant the considerable investment in carrying out the procedures which will be described.

Objectives-Based Systems Analysis

In most systems analysis models there are three sets of questions to be answered. These questions are associated with the three major phases of managing a system, as follows:

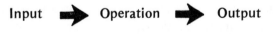

Input ➡ Operation ➡ Output

A Simplified System Model

There are questions regarding which *inputs* should be made to the system, that is, the purposes for which the system exists and the types of resources which will be used to attain those purposes. A second set of questions is associated with the actual *operation* of the system, that is, how well are things working? A final group of questions stems from an appraisal of the *output* of the system, that is, was the effectiveness of the system such that it should remain essentially unmodified or do we have to make some changes in it?

There is nothing inherent in systems analysis models which requires one to employ instructional objectives as an organizing rubric in the implementation of a model. There may be preferable classification schemes for organizing the data which must be processed in a systems analysis scheme. The present paper, however, will be addressed to a systems analysis strategy in which instructional objectives play a prominent role. The choice to employ objectives as the organizing dimension stems from a belief that statements of instructional objectives can serve as a parsimonious vehicle for communicating the information which must be considered at various points in analyzing the system. Note, for instance, that those individuals operating the National Assessment of Educational Progress, surely dealing with a large-scale educational enterprise, have chosen to employ statements of instructional objectives as their organizing rubric.

A learner's status in connection with an educational system may be represented by his or her performance on an examination of some sort. Rather than requiring a decision-maker to scrutinize the entire examination, we may convey an idea of what the examination entails by identifying the learner competencies it was designed to measure. Often these competencies can be described as a *desired* status for the learner, hence the equivalent of an instructional objective. In addition, many educators are quite familiar with the general concept of instructional objectives, this topic having received ample attention during the past decade.

To reiterate, it is not requisite to employ instructional objectives as the organizing theme for an educational systems analysis model. Nonetheless, the use of objectives for this purpose seems to offer some advantages and, accordingly, the remainder of this paper will describe a systems model for large educational enterprises which prominently employs instructional objectives.

Measurable Objectives

It is important to note at the outset of this discussion that, unless otherwise noted, we will employ the phrase "instructional objective" to represent a *measurable* instructional objective. Because measurable objectives communicate one's instructional intentions with less ambiguity than broad, general objectives, it would seem particularly important to use such objectives in a rational decision-making scheme where any extra system noise (such as ambiguous symbology) will reduce the quality of the decisions. In recent years, of course, there have been numerous treatises written regarding technical questions of how such measurable objectives should be optimally formulated.

Returning now to the general questions which an educational systems analyst must attempt to answer, we can turn first to what is perhaps the most important question facing any systems designer. This question is, "To what ends should the system be committed?" Putting it another way, "Why should the education system be there in the first place?" For an objectives-based systems analysis approach, this essentially becomes the problem of goal determination.

Goal Determination

In general, the proponent of systems analysis approaches subscribes to a classic means/ends paradigm. It is anticipated that if proper ends can be identified it will be worth the trouble to test the efficacy of alternative means to achieve those ends until certain means can be identified which do the job. In the field of education we are becoming increasingly more sophisticated in designing instructional sequences. It thus becomes increasingly imperative to identify the most defensible goals of our educational systems so that improved instructional means can be directed toward the proper ends.

There are at least two approaches to specifying the appropriate objectives for a large-scale educational system, and these are somewhat analogous to an inductive versus a deductive approach. Characteristically, we have employed an inductive strategy over the years in education. According to this scheme, the educational planner consults various groups with a series of general questions such as "What do you want our schools to accomplish?" People typically respond to such questions with varying degrees of specificity, so it is usually up to the educational planner to synthesize their somewhat diffuse reactions and translate them into more or less definitive goal statements. Ralph Tyler's curriculum model, which has, at least at a theoretical level, been quite influential during the past several decades, represents such an approach.

An alternative attack upon the goal determination problem has become available in recent years through the establishment of large pools of measurable instructional objectives. Various clienteles can rate objectives from these pools as to the appropriateness of their inclusion in the curriculum of a given education system. In this latter approach, therefore, we do not try to derive statements of objectives from the value preferences and informal assertions of people; rather, we present people with objectives from which they choose those they consider most important.

Perhaps because the latter approach seems to offer a greater possibility of systematization through technical refinement, it has received more attention during recent months. Particularly as a consequence of the *needs assessment* operations required by federal ESEA Title III funding programs, we find more and more educators who are attempting to rigorously establish objectives for large-scale educational endeavors. A number of these efforts have involved the use of deductively designated educational objectives.

The general strategy in an objectives-based goal determination operation involves presentation of alternative sets of educational objectives to groups who have a stake in deciding what the goals of the system ought to be. These groups then rate, rank, or in other ways display their preferences regarding those objectives. The expressed preferences of the various groups are then surveyed by those who must ultimately decide on the system's goals and, hopefully, more enlightened judgments regarding what the system's goals ought to be can be made on the basis of such preference data.

The somewhat new feature of this approach to goal determination involves the use of measurable objectives. In previous efforts to employ this general strategy, educators often used loose, nonmeasurable goals which almost served as Rorschach inkblots for those expressing their preferences; that is, people read into nebulous goal statements almost anything they wished. As a consequence, it was extremely difficult to make reasonable contrasts among the preferences of various groups. With the use of measurable objectives, fortunately, ambiguity is reduced, and as a consequence differences among various clienteles are more directly a function of their real differences in values, rather than of confusion regarding the meaning of certain goal statements.

The kinds of groups which might be involved, of course, will vary from one educational enterprise to another. For instance, in the California higher education evaluation system, it would seem imperative to involve student groups from the various types of higher education institutions within the state, that is, community colleges, state colleges, and universities. It would seem equally important to involve citizen groups of various kinds, e.g., parents, businessmen, and other public-spirited citizens. This would be an ideal opportunity, for example, to secure preference inputs from ethnic and other minority groups who often feel large educational systems are unresponsive to their particular curricular preferences. It might be particularly appropriate to secure the reactions of a group of specially designated *futurists*, whose charge would be to consider higher education objectives in light of their suitability for the 1980s and 1990s, not merely for the next few years. The preferences of these groups can be coalesced and represented in straightforward numerical form in any one of several methods. If at any point in the goal determination operation it is discovered that important goals have been overlooked, they can be easily added to the array of objectives to be rated.

To illustrate an alternative, somewhat less quantitative, method of establishing priorities among competing objectives, Professor Robert E. Stake of the University of Illinois has recently devised an approach to priorities planning in which the decision-makers consider data such as the preferences of various clienteles. However, they also survey the system's requisite resource allocations, the payoff probabilities of various objectives, and the relevant contingency conditions, that is, special circumstances which might call for change in instructional procedures.

Having established the preferred objectives of a system, an important second step in the goal determination is to discover the degree to which the target learners can already display the hoped-for behaviors designated by the various reference groups. This is where measurable instructional objectives offer considerable advantages, for since the objectives which have been rated by the various groups are stated in explicit and measurable terms, it is a relatively straightforward task to devise measuring devices from those objectives and, as a consequence, to measure the learner's status.

We would certainly employ item and person sampling techniques in this approach in order to conserve testing time and to make the task economically feasible. But, by using such techniques, whereby only certain students are sampled and those sampled complete only segments of the total measuring devices, we can certainly measure student attainment of the high priority goals established via the previous rating/ranking procedure.

The next step, then, is to contrast the learners' status with the high-priority goals and decide which of these we wish to direct our educational enterprise toward. Clearly, there are still a great many value judgments to be made at this point, but the hope is that by making the decisions as heavily data-based as possible, superior decisions will be made.

One of the more persistent problems having to do with

the technology of objectives concerns the *level of generality* of those objectives. Individuals working with instructional objectives since Ralph Tyler's early efforts have pointed out that the level of specificity question or, conversely, the level of generality issue is one of the most important questions to be resolved in the field of instructional objectives. Yet no one seems to have come up with a very satisfactory solution. Our general estimate at this point, however, is that we must find some way to present larger "chunks" of educational objectives to various groups for ratings. Ending up with more than twenty-five or thirty objectives which must be rated presents, to most humans, an unmanageable intellectual task.

It is interesting to note that in certain relatively large school districts in the State of California the number of reading objectives has been reduced to only three or four; thus a single objective, e.g., a student's ability to decode twenty-five words randomly drawn from a list of 500, serves to represent the bulk of that district's reading effort.

It is quite apparent that more attention must be given to the matter of how general an objective should be in order for it to prove serviceable in this type of situation.

Progress Monitoring

The second set of questions of concern to those involved in decisions regarding educational systems concerns the appraisal of the progress of the system toward its stipulated goals. One relatively straightforward method of discerning the degree to which the system's goals are being accomplished involves the administration of criterion-referenced tests associated with the various system goals so that indications of learner progress toward those goals can be secured. Goals which, according to measured learner progress, are not being achieved can be attacked with alternative instructional strategies, additional resources, etc. Goals which are being achieved on schedule permit the inference that the instructional program is working as well as needed. It is even conceivable, of course, that some goals will be achieved ahead of schedule, thereby permitting a shifting of resources toward less effective instructional activities.

It is at this juncture that the evaluator should be particularly attentive to unanticipated consequences of the educational system's operation. Whereas educational designers can spell out carefully the hoped-for outcomes of an educational enterprise, it is often the case that some unintended and aversive consequences ensue which were simply unforeseen by the instructional designers.

Output Appraisal

The final set of questions regarding the management of a large-scale educational system concerns the final quality of its results. Once more, since we are using objectives as an organizing rubric, it is possible to develop criterion-referenced tests which are congruent with those objectives and administer them on a matrix sampling basis to the learners served by the system. Results on such measures, combined with measures of unanticipated consequences, will yield the kind of evidence necessary to reach a judgment regarding the quality of the educational enterprise.

A particularly thorny problem arises related to the manner in which results of such an analysis should be reported. Educational evaluators are only now beginning to wrestle seriously with alternative vehicles for reporting evaluative results in such a way that decision-makers can take appropriate action based on the evaluation data. All too frequently we find evaluation endeavors resulting in encyclopedic final reports which only a person of great devotion has the patience to read completely. Brevity is a desirable criterion in reporting results of evaluation studies irrespective of the type of evaluation report involved.

Again, the organizing theme for evaluation, at least for the approach being described here, would be the use of instructional objectives. Progress toward the major instructional objectives adopted by the educational system would be reported to the appropriate decision-making groups, e.g., local school boards, state school boards, university regents, etc. In a general before-after model it is important to present the data in as succinct a fashion as possible so that those utilizing the results can make more sense out of them. Here is where the educational evaluator will have to be particularly judicious in the data he selects to report and the manner in which those data are described.

Theory and Practice

In the foregoing paragraphs a general strategy for the management of large educational enterprises has been described. Clearly, the discussion has been at a very general level. Sometimes one has the feeling that in propounding a given theoretical point of view, an effort to implement it in practice will result in chaos. The technical problems are seen as too serious to work out.

With present propositions, however, this does not seem to be the case. Surely there will be technical and procedural questions which must be dealt with. For example, exactly which groups will be involved in rating the objectives that will result in the selection of goals for the system? How many learners should be tested in order to yield reasonable estimates regarding the progress of the system as well as its final output? What kinds of departures from anticipated progress should dictate modifications in the system? These and other problems can be faced and, I believe, resolved by individuals wishing to seriously monitor the progress of a large-scale educational enterprise.

But that kind of operation takes more money than most educators have been willing to spend. Other than the recently initiated Experimental Schools Program of the U.S. Office of Education, we see few large-scale educational enterprises in which ample funds have been set aside for evaluation. Most state and local school systems operate under an explicit evaluation budget of less than one percent, if that much. The kind of evaluation endeavor we are talking about here clearly will demand resources of around five percent or better. The first-blush reluctance of individuals to spend that kind of money should be countered by hard-nosed estimates of the benefits, both economic and educational, which can be derived from rigorously evaluating the progress of a large-scale educational undertaking. The costs of ineffectual instruction are enormous.

Perfection and Imperfectibility

Some detractors will allege quite accurately that systems approaches such as those described here are laden with flaws. Surely by using objectives-based systems we will discover that certain critical features of the educational system are not appraised with sufficient sensitivity to yield the right kind of information for making proper decisions. When faced with these kinds of criticism, however, I am reminded that decisions must currently be made regarding educational enterprises, day in and day out. And at the moment these decisions are being made with far less sophistication, far less data, and far less accuracy than might be rendered under a system such as that proposed herein. Granted that a systems analysis approach is not perfect, it nevertheless seems to offer a clear improvement over the general quality of decision-making seen so prevalently these days in educational arenas. And, perhaps more importantly, because of its systematic nature, such an approach is amenable to technical self-correction and, over time, incremental improvement—so that even if the management system lacks total perfection, it will be so close that the learners it serves won't know the difference.

3

The Limits of Scientific-Economic-Technological Approaches and the Search for Perspective in Education: The Case of Performance Contracting

Albert H. Yee

> The *Titanic* woke them up. Never again would they be quite
> so sure of themselves. In technology especially, the disaster
> was a terrible blow. Here was the "unsinkable ship"—per-
> haps man's greatest engineering achievement—going down
> the first time it sailed.
>
> Walter Lord
> *A Night to Remember*

In later years, we shall recall accountability and performance contracting as two of the most important educational concepts of the early 1970s. Seldom have key concepts
found educational decision-makers so supportive and been
better representative of the attitude and philosophy of the
times. Receiving much discussion in lay and professional
writings, mostly favorable and noncontentious, they are
undergoing a climactic turning point at the present time. For
performance contracting, educational management's pet
stratagem to accountability and educational revolution, has
recently failed some crucial tests of its effectiveness.

In 1972, the Office of Economic Opportunity completed a $7.2 million study of performance contracting it had
conducted independently with 18 urban and rural school

systems and six contractors during the 1970-71 school year. Without any mincing of words, OEO (1972) reported that the performance of performance contracting was a failure:

> The results of the experiment clearly indicate that the firms operating under performance contracts did not perform significantly better than the more traditional school systems. Indeed, both control and experimental students did equally poorly in terms of achievement gains, and this result was remarkably consistent across sites and among children with different degrees of initial capability . . . It is clear that there is no evidence to support a massive move to utilize performance contracting for remedial education in the nation's schools. School districts should be skeptical of extravagant claims for the concept . . . it is clearly another failure in our search for means of helping poor and disadvantaged youngsters to develop the skills they need to lift themselves out of poverty (pp. 31-32).

OEO reports that only two of the participating contractors in their experiment continue to operate. One contractor, Behavioral Research Laboratories, has seen the price of its stock fall from more than $20.00 per share to the area of $5.00 per share. In the no-nonsense business world where profitability and performance supposedly count, the plain fact is that performance contractors are not surviving. The educational and financial evidence to date, which might be least affected by the Hawthorne effect, indicates that performance contracting cannot fulfill its glorified image.

Proponents, however, insist that they have or will have favorable evidence, though little has been made available to counter findings such as OEO's. Amidst such developments, therefore, perspective concerning performance contracting and its assumptions seems highly pertinent.

First, what is the rationale for performance contracting? According to one of its top spokesmen (Lessinger, 1970), "The principle of public accountability is the key to the adoption of educational engineering, for in order to answer to the public in terms of results, school officials will have to adopt certain managerial procedures that both stimulate the demand for performance and help them provide it (pp. 30-31)."

To accomplish the goal, school administrators (i.e., school managers) are instructed to do (i.e., engineer) all of the basic things that have been familiar in pedagogy, such as defining objectives in measurable terms and interrelating school and community. However, the single new factor is modifying the administrative structure and operation of schooling through contracts with profit-motivated private firms independent of the schools, which our advocate defines as follows:

> Essentially, a performance contract is an agreement by a firm or individual to produce specified results by a certain date, using acceptable methods, for a set fee. The parties may agree in advance that, if the conditions are not met by that date, the firm must continue its efforts, for no additional fee, until they are met; and also that if the requirements are exceeded, either by early completion or by a higher level of achievement, the fee will be

increased by specified amounts. Thus, in a contract for educational services, the school has a guarantee that for the budgeted expenditure, students will acquire certain skills, as measured by an independent auditor; and the supplier of the services has a strong incentive not only to meet but to exceed the contractual requirements (Lessinger, 1970, p. 18).

The stress upon material values in the quote cannot be missed.

Much of the support for performance contracting stems from legitimate concern over school costs and the need to meet the accountability challenge. National opinion surveys (e.g., Gallup, 1971) indicate that many educational analysts and decision-makers believe that performance contracting can cut school costs and achieve solid results. For many administrators and school boards, it became their salvation against many troublesome and contradictory demands, such as those of the disadvantaged, contract negotiations with teachers, the mounting pressure of frustrated taxpayers, and the overall inadequacies of a sick and complex system. Presenting rather pedestrian assertions about what ails the educational process and simplifying issues to narrow terms, e.g., "no results, no pay," the advocates of performance contracting deserve critique in at least three areas: 1) the methods by which results are evaluated, 2) the adequacy of the scientific-economic-technological framework for educational decision-making, and 3) the nature of teacher-learner relations.

First, the point where one evaluates and determines performance failure or success is the weakest single element of the whole scheme. Others (Klein, 1971; Schutz, 1971; Ward, 1970) have already critiqued the testing problems in performance contracting, so present comments on this point can be brief.

Almost everyone knows about the Texarkana incident where the contractor was said to have taught to the tests. Just how performance contracting as it is now conceived can overcome the problem of evaluating results without undue reliance upon tests remains an open question. The mind boggles over the diverse machinations that school authorities, teachers, contractors, and pupils might use to manipulate test scores one way or the other. For example, will tax-paying parents think twice about asking their children to do as well as they can on posttests? Also, there seems to have been little concern about experimenter effects on test subjects and performance contracting (e.g., Kennedy and Vega, 1971; Sattler, 1970).

Advocates of performance contracting have not responded well to the testing problems, such as regression effects and invalid grade-equivalent scores. The few attempts to explain how testing can be made feasible for performance contracting are circuitous, to say the least. They offer nothing new in defining what dependent measures will be adequate for the kinds of analysis and decisions that concise accountability requires, such as are possible in specifying the performance of machines. Classifying the independent variables is fairly simple, but one proponent (Barro, 1970) could only describe the dependent variables as follows: "Specific measurement instruments to be used and dimensions of performance to be measured would have to be determined by individual school systems in accordance with their educational objectives. No attempt will be made here to specify what items should be included (p. 201)." A footnote mentioned standardized reading and cognitive tests as well as attendance data, but saying there are "innumerable possibilities" seems to beg the question in light of the purposes intended.

The common rule for educational assessment and decision-making on the basis of test results requires knowledgeable precautions and tolerance for slippage; but it is a whole new ballgame when the profit motive becomes involved in the use of tests. As Ward (1970) puts it, "Tests should be a *reflection* of what is important, rather than a *determiner* of what is important for boys and girls to learn (p. 3)." Even if adequate tests existed, performance contracting's constant demand for concise and absolute tests of effectiveness cannot help but influence what will and will not be taught.

Predictably, there has been overemphasis on rote and skills learning in the content areas under contract as well as the vitiating stress on extrinsic motivators—candy, transistor radios, comics, and free time in "Reinforcing Environment" lounge centers stocked with games and other goodies. Compared to the rhetoric of proponents about teacher and pupil apathy, such rewards for children seem shallow indeed. How long will it take the kids to realize their test scores must improve before teachers and contractors get paid and begin to hustle the educators for a real "cut of the bread" (Saretsky, 1971)? Such are the dangers of simplex and hasty approaches. In comparison, the modest assumptions, aims, and painstaking design and methodology of the National Assessment of Educational Progress project provide an Ariel-Caliban contrast.

SET Approaches to Social Policy

Moving on, performance contracting also becomes involved in the rationale of the scientific-economic-technological (SET) frame of reference so predominant in modern life, and in the issue of its limits in social policy and practice. The SET frame that I will discuss at length includes the assumptions of empiricism in which, as Popper (1959, p. 59) put it: "The empirical sciences are systems of theories . . . (which) are nets cast to catch what we call 'the world': to rationalize, to explain, and to master it. We endeavour to make the mesh ever finer and finer." The frame also includes supplementary economic-management sciences or systems analysis which help to formulate rational solutions to specific, predesignated problems by keying upon selected facts and prediction to one-time events (Schaeffer, *et al.*, 1963). In education, the rational SET approach has been described as consisting of a series of logical steps, such as in Project ARISTOTLE (Lehmann, 1968):

1.   Statement of need and importance
2.   Specification of behavioral objectives
3.   Constraints to be considered
4.   Survey of alternative approaches
5.   Selection of the best alternative
6.   Implementation of required operations
7.   Evaluation of results
8.   Modification for improvement

Such basic steps comprise a familiar formula that pervades much of modern education. Following one or more of the various taxonomies of behavior, we are supposed to define and pursue specific objectives in behavioral terms so we know with a minimum of equivocality what is to be learned, how it will be taught and evaluated, etc. In the overall view of organizational management, school processes are systematized from broad to minute parts with "primary responsibility for the design of the curriculum and instructional subsystems . . . (assumed) outside the schools" and with reward made proportional to effort and recognized contributions to efficiency (Bushnell, 1971).

In general, such views seem to make good sense, for it can be argued that education, wherever it may be found, implies purpose, organization, and effective teaching-learning processes. Curricular differences can be largely analyzed by the decisions and assumptions underlying them to guide what education is to accomplish and why, how schools and classes will be organized to achieve the desired effects, and the general nature of actual instruction and learning to influence students. Therefore, schools by definition are purposeful, operational systems that lend themselves fairly well to broad and rational analysis. However, the crucial questions are: who makes the decisions, how are they reached, on what set of criteria, and with how much control and specification of goals and results?

Promotion and use of SET management processes by big government, business, science, and industry began to influence educational decision-makers during the Johnson administration. Ever-increasing centralization of administrative control over schools fostered the climate and conditions for the development of an educational "power elite," akin to what C. Wright Mills (1956) found in those very same fields that developed the management systems approach. Unfortunately, as systematic processes began to appear in education, analysts and decision-makers with greater experience with systems approaches in other fields were beginning to sense unexpected shortcomings in them.

Can we deny the existence of social attitudes and how importantly a society's orientation to human values influences its thinking and behavior, now that we can begin to take perspective on the 1960s? Decision-makers of the 1960s expressed great optimism and self-assured arrogance in their belief that rational prescriptions for the improvement of society could be designed and implemented—to eradicate poverty, improve the economy, and devise complex, fail-safe defense systems. Such a belief meshed well with popular consensus and political matters, and sophisticated SET tools and management systems (which proliferated during WW II and the Korean War) seemed so obviously conducive to the fulfillment of public policy and solution of social issues. That was the era when LBJ called for the "Great Society" and said we could have "guns and butter" at the same time, when graduating engineers, scientists, and mathematicians could pick and choose among many job offers, and when the SET rationale was the public rationale. The image of the intelligent, dedicated decision-maker was auto magnate and Defense Secretary Robert S. McNamara. Perceived as seeking and displaying maximum objectivity and detachment, McNamara's classic pose was poring over explicit analyses of the needs, alternatives, and costs portrayed in elaborate flowcharts.

Describing the Defense Department's use of the Planning-Programming-Budgeting System (PPBS), the Defense Secretary's top analysts, Enthoven and Smith (1971, p. 47), wrote:

The fundamental idea behind PPBS was decision-making based on explicit criteria related to the national interest in defense programs as opposed to decision-making by compromise among various institutional and parochial interests. PPBS also emphasized the consideration of real alternatives, the importance of evaluating needs and costs together, the need for a multi-year force and financial plan, the regular use of an analytical staff as an aid to decision-makers at the top levels, and the importance of making analyses open and explicit. These were the basic ideas underlying PPBS and the management tools that made the system work.

However, no matter how objective and religiously developed management techniques such as PPBS became, they could not avoid subjective values and judgments. Rational analysis, as exemplified by Defense Secretary McNamara's mastery, failed in many tragic ways (*Time*, 1971b). No matter how extensively his analyses and alternatives were displayed and scrutinized, fatal decisions concerning Vietnam and weapon systems were based primarily on political and intuitive judgments. The decisions fitted decision trees as neatly as their opposite response would have fitted, as one throws electric switches one way or the other. The Pentagon papers tragically show that, and why there must be greater open debate and interrogation of military strategy and needs involving independent analysts, Congress, and the public.

It is better realized today that the systematic approach in and of itself cannot make the crucial decisions. Analyses based only on minute reductionism often made decision-making more difficult, decreased flexibility and the generation of alternatives, made it more costly to relinquish prior commitments, only tolerated innovations that "added-on," and lessened open and balanced debate. SET processes are means, a series of means, but never ends (Ferkiss, 1969). A journalist (Bartley, 1971) wrote: "If it is understood, rigorous rational analysis can strip away illusions. But if the ultimately intuitive element is overlooked or obscured, the same analysis can create illusions; it can be so helpful in our efforts to persuade ourselves we know more than we do." As Enthoven and Smith (1971, p. 64) put it, "The point of analysis is not to give the answer, but rather to show how the answer depends on various assumptions and judgments. In any analysis, the assumptions drive the conclusions. There can be no doubt about that nor about the fact that there is no single 'right' set of assumptions, but only a variety of sets of relevant assumptions, each more or less equally defensible."

President Kennedy's decision to go to the moon (Logsdon, 1970; Mandelbaum, 1969) illustrates the rationale of the 1960s and how SET approaches were used to justify and implement political and intuitive decisions. Blankenship (1971) described the $20 billion commitment to the moon as follows:

> (The decision) . . . captured the mood of America at the time; that it was a politically neutral project and fitted well a system of values in which technology and competitiveness are equated with progress and strength; that there was something in it for most of the influential or prestigious institutions and groups in American society: the Congress, private industry, universities, the scientific and engineering communities, unions and blue-

collar workers, the mass media, especially tele-
vision, the banks, and the military; that it related
to a delimited goal that could be understood and
achieved with existing scientific knowledge; that it
was backed up by an unusually competent management team and a highly dedicated group of rocket
scientists (p. 318).

Hopeful that they too can find the proper facility and
solution, educators have typically sought utopia through
some SET process, especially in a one- or two-variable design
that can be justified with the simplest conceptual frame. We
have had proposals to pay parents and teachers for pupil
achievement, calm pupils with drugs, and differentiate
instruction on the basis of crude racial-SES classifications.
There are the claims and counter-claims for all kinds of
super-solutions—reading achievement through the processes
of neurological maturation, teaching machines, busing,
modular scheduling, schools without walls, school vouchers,
CAI, etc. We see the basic problem of over-simplification in
the words of Behavioral Research Laboratories' school
manager in Gary, Indiana: "We want a job done (likening
education to the assembly line). One fellow puts in the nuts,
you put in the bolts, and the product comes out (*Time*,
1971a)."

In general agreement with Ellul's (1964) sobering
critique of technological society, I would not go so far as to
imply, however, that the problem lies so much in the
techniques themselves; for the important question about
them is why, not how. Techniques must always be regarded
as means to fundamental long-range values concerning the
individual and social living. One gets the feeling that the

ultimate outcome of the strict SET approach to social policy will be totalitarianism and irrespect for individuality. And one senses too that, as its basic nature cannot be modified to overcome the problem of means and ends, there must be complementary approaches and procedures.

With special reference to Project Camelot, the largest federally supported project in the social sciences and perhaps the most highly publicized clash of political and SET values, Vallance (1972) argued that the conduct of the social sciences, basic or applied, always impinges on human values and attitudes. While concerned scientists, such as Vallance, accept methodology or techniques as being mostly value-free, they focus their concern upon the use of techniques, e.g., the "process of intervening in the lives and institutional organizations of people, and the overriding ethical problems in managing a someday truly successful social science (Vallance, 1972, p. 108)." Illustrating how progress proceeds from how to why, computer-assisted instruction attracted much attention and support during the 1960s because of three main factors: 1) development of programmed instruction, 2) expanding capability of electronic data processing, and 3) increasing federal support of educational research and development (Atkinson and Wilson, 1968).

Thoughtful attempts to confront such problems by devising clever methodological techniques and involving scientists more completely in social change experiments (Campbell, 1969) do not satisfy the basic problems. Shaver and Staines (1972) raised a number of specific "practical, political, theoretical, and ethical questions still to be resolved" in Campbell's proposed "experimenting society" and concluded that "methodological virtuosity on its own . . . will not resolve all the problems (p. 163)." Campbell's (1972) recent reply indicates some agreement, especially the point that objectivity and solution for the problems can be best obtained through "competitive scrutiny" by partisans of relevant contrasting views. Noted scientists, such as Jerome Wiesner and Herbert York, have said that the dilemma of the arms race has no technical solution and to seek solutions in science and technology would only worsen the situation (Ferry, 1968). Technology assessment by a watchguard federal agency, as has been proposed by Congressman E.Q. Daddario's Subcommittee on Science, Research and Development and the National Academy of Sciences (Brooks and Bowers, 1970) may prove to be useful. But it alone would be quite insufficient until more scientists consider the broader social consequences of their work.

Scientists who maintain the traditional attitude that science can be value-free and detached often indicate unawareness that they may be overstating the case for SET approaches. According to Schon (1971), there is a SET management approach to about every problem, from the laundry industry and urban ghettoes to reading and revolution, and that any social phenomenon from dyadic interaction to the general "youth movement" can be analyzed and handled with the rational/experimental model, as defined by Hainer's (1968) description of rationalism and pragmatism. Though his technical procedures seem feasible, Skinner's (1971) attempts to argue the comprehensive approach to human freedom and dignity through the greater scientific control of man and environment are unconvincing, if not disturbing:

> Science does not dehumanize man, it de-homunculizes him, and it must do so if it is to prevent the

abolition of the human species. To man *qua* man
we readily say good riddance. Only by dispossess-
ing him can we turn to the real causes of human
behavior. Only then can we turn from the inferred
to the observed, from the miraculous to the
natural, from the inaccessible to the manipulable
(pp. 200-201).

The AAAS Committee on Sciences in the Promotion of
Human Welfare (*Educational Researcher*, 1972) recently
observed that scientists have not wanted or been able to
influence social policy decision-making. Their passivity comes
from not realizing their larger role, their lack of needed
background and ability to make policy decisions, and
willingness to be called and serve after administrative
decisions have been made. As a HUD official put it:
"Hearings are merely window-dressing to provide some
technical data on one side or the other . . . . Scientists too
often assume that someone else must be taking care of the
fire (p. 18)."

Reacting against the traditional attitude toward science,
more and more scientists express belief that the strict SET
approach itself is not omnipotent and all-encompassing. Such
scientists see that the quantifying, detached posture of the
scientist is unrealistic, that believing it is possible has
produced contradictory consequences and made him a
partner in the use of science for exploitative and destructive
purposes (Beals, 1969; Blackburn, 1971; Brooks, 1971;
Brown, 1971; Horowitz, 1971; Kelman, 1968). A noted
biologist (Morison, 1969) described the growing negative
attitudes among young intellectuals, scientists, and the public
as "skepticism about rational systems" in general. It is far less

popular today to accept Bacon's aphorism that we cannot command nature except by obeying her. While few persons once questioned the "splendid idealism" of science, as expressed by Sinclair Lewis' characterization of Dr. Gottleib and Arrowsmith (Schorer, 1961, p. 417), such characters seem quite outdated and unreal today.

Many now realize that science and technology have never been what their images intended (e.g., Beveridge, 1957; Thorson, 1970). Morison (1969) wrote:

> Too often we conjure up genies who produce short-term benefits at the risk of much larger long-term losses. We develop marvelous individual transport systems which poison the air we breathe; learn how to make paper very cheaply at the cost of ruining our rivers; and fabricate weapons that determine our defense strategy and foreign policy rather than being determined by them. Above all, the applications of science have produced an unrestricted increase in the human population which we recognize as fatal to our welfare but have only the vaguest idea how to control. In a short time we will be able to design the genetic structure of a good man. There is some uncertainty about the exact date, but no doubt that it will come before we have defined what a good man is (p. 154).

With the advantages of being insiders, concerned scientists find many current examples and assumptions to challenge in defense and ecology. In those areas, obvious negative first- and/or second-order effects are apparent enough to the average person, but the greater opportunity to influence change may be the scientist's, such as occurred during the SST debates.

Education's Need for Reassessment and New Approaches

Reassessing assumptions in professional education, especially with intervention designs such as performance contracting, would be very healthy. Have we been as committed to the good, the true, and the beautiful as we would want? If we say that at least we have been in search of the truth, if not moral and aesthetic concerns because of methodological constraints, why is it that our colleagues in the arts and humanities are not alone in viewing research journals in the educational and social sciences as being generally "full of formalistic exercises in methodology" in which scientific rigor and detachment are pursued to the "point of disinterest" and "useless trivia" (Rapping and Rapping, 1968, p. 76)? Such critics are not only unimpressed with scientific rigor and esoterica, they also question the motives of social scientists, who appear to them to be more committed to the status quo and the interests of funding agencies than objective detachment and public policy (Nisbet, 1971).

As one examines the inevitable methodological debate following a critical study (e.g., the Coleman Report) or surrounding a controversial issue (e.g., debate involving Black, Platt, Skinner, and Toynbee on the topic "Beyond Freedom and Dignity?" *Center Magazine*, 1972), the assumptions concerning the omnipotence and truthability of SET approaches often seem inflated and unrealistic. Examining various approaches to process classroom observations, Yamamoto, Jones, and Ross (1972) found that conflicting conclusions can be drawn from the same data by way of the particular method of data reduction. Thus, they urged us "not to ignore the peculiarly personal basis of scientific knowledge itself" and to realize that topics of relevance begin and end as matters of judgment. The stimulating Gage-Jensen-Shockley debate on heritability and educational potential in the January and March 1972 issues of the *Phi Delta Kappan* bears out such advice. Concerned with the consequences of one line of "scientific" claims that are not final but can be used to suit negative conclusions, Gage (1972) wrote: "I agree that the intellectual community has a moral obligation to think. That obligation should weigh heavily on those who attribute black disadvantages to genetic factors and despair of environmental attacks upon them (p. 427)."

Writing earlier on the same issue, Boyer and Walsh (1968, p. 78, italics theirs) stated: *"Lacking definitive scientific evidence about human potentialities, social policy should be based on moral considerations. We should base our policy on the most generous and promising assumptions about human nature rather than the most niggardly and pessimistic . . . (Both sets of assumptions) about human nature create their own self-fulfilling prophecies."* Can scientific and moral considerations ever be properly separate and distinct in education?

Each educator should reflect upon his perspective and see if there is not an over-commitment to a frame of reference for schools that is narrower and simpler than desired. We might ask, what would schools and society look like if SET methods and assumptions were successfully implemented? Granted we are limited to what is observable, and united we stand against vague verbiage; but in our haste to achieve short-term performance gains and greater control with narrow means, what far-reaching human values and potentials have we negated? One outcome of our present approaches is that school achievement seems to be negatively correlated to the attitudes of pupils toward learning and school. Even if we just wanted to hedge our bets a little, just in case there is something to these concerns, we might try to be less cocksure of our assumptions that SET approaches are fully instrumental.

Differing approaches need not be in conflict but could operate with something like the notion of complementarity that physicist Niels Bohr (1963) proposed. Forced to expand the frame of reference of classical physics to accommodate the observational problem of atomic physics, Bohr felt that nature could only be described by viewing sensuous and rational knowledge and aesthetic and quantitative valuations as complementary processes, each retaining its own integrity. Speaking to the same issue, Oppenheimer (1953) wrote that even if the "physical correlate of elements of consciousness" should be found, it would not appropriately describe:

> the thinking man himself, for the clarification of his thoughts, the resolution of his will, or the delight of his eye and mind are works of beauty. Indeed, an understanding of the complementary nature of conscious life and its physical interpretation appears to me a lasting element in human understanding and a proper formulation of the historic views called psycho-physical parallelism (p. 81).

With particular reference to the social and biological sciences, Bohr argued that all experience, whether in science, philosophy, or art, must be pursued to develop a meaningful unity of knowledge. "Anxiously aware that the power to change is not always necessarily good" and with immense trust in human freedom and diversity, Oppenheimer (1953) called for a "unity of science . . . that is far more a unity of comparable dedication than a unity of common total understanding" where separate contexts, ideas, and approaches might help expand the other, not for a "global or total or hierarchical" absolute unity of mind and community (pp. 95-97).

Speaking to psychologists, Oppenheimer (1956) spoke of analogies that help explain things because they provide structural parallels from essentially diverse views. From modern physics' view of "individuality, wholeness, the subtle relations of what is seen with how it is seen, the indeterminacy and the acausality of experience (p. 134)," Oppenheimer cautioned psychologists not to take narrow, rigid approaches and urged them not to overemphasize quantification. Saying "it is not always clear that by measuring one has found something very worth measuring," he said quantification alone was not the best way "to advance true understanding of what is going on" and made a "very strong plea for pluralism with regard to methods" of explanation and a "minimal definition of objectivity (p. 135)." Disciplined inquiry in education, according to a report of the Committee on Educational Research of the National Academy of Education (Cronbach and Suppes, 1969), "requires nonquantitative as well as quantitative techniques" and should not be narrowly restricted to quantitative procedures. Krantz (1972) has recently argued the same general point as he discussed the relation of measurement to the development and testing of qualitative psychological laws. He wrote: "The danger . . . lies in the fact that for many substantive areas of psychology, there is absolutely no reason to expect qualitative laws leading to measurement structures. *The goal of scientific psychology is not measurement, but theory. And theory comes in various and unexpected forms* (italics mine, p. 1434)."

Another great physicist, Gell-Mann (1971), recently described the negative effects of and attacked narrow rationality:

> that takes into account in decision-making only things that are very easy to quantify, and sets equal to zero things that are hard to quantify. But sometimes those latter things are of paramount importance, like beauty or diversity or the irreversibility of change, in the case of the environment; like privacy for the individual; for our institutions, an analog is the quality of giving people the feeling that they are in control of the rapid change that is occurring in their world. We see narrow rationality in the making of some government decisions of great importance. We see facts and figures marshalled in huge arrays that have failed somehow to include inputs from common sense or from human values (p. 23).

It seems ironic that Nobel Laureates in physics should decry today's practices of systems analysis and over-concern with reductionism. They certainly know what SET processes can produce and do to the world. When they say "the priority need is to develop a systems analysis with heart that society can rely on to choose between possible technologies" and develop more modest and intrusive technology as far as the environment and individual is concerned (Gell-Mann, 1971, p. 23), nuclear physicists might know what they are saying.

Such views of science require greater interdisciplinary approaches. The various analytical approaches to atomistic and quantitative precision in goal achievement must become complemented one with the other and with the various synthesizing approaches for global and essential significance in human values. Isolation and separate approaches have seemed to be easier than working together. Seeking a unity of knowledge, however, would not necessarily mean common agreement in all matters nor acceptance of anything. In an open, balanced debate of views, greater synthesis will develop and judgments should improve.

Calling for an "open pluralism of strategy" that is directly concerned with human values, Smith (1969) wrote:

> One may entertain different grades of evidence without being misled—so long as we remain critically aware of its limitations. One may glean insights and hypotheses from many sources, including common human experience and its refinement in the arts, later to be tested by firmer criteria. I am convinced that there is no royal road to Truth, not even that of the experimentalist. Truth is elusive, and we do best to converge upon it from multiple perspectives (p. 7).

Educational research is often perceived as being synonymous with statistical significance, and that is just not right. It clearly reflects narrow over-specialization in our thinking and formal training, but educational scholars are not alone. Addressing himself to social psychological research, Smith (1969) regretted the overemphasis upon laboratory experimentation and the decline of synthesizing approaches. He wrote: " . . . virtuosity rather than substance seems to have carried the day: manipulative virtuosity in the laboratory, and theoretical virtuosity in experimentally armed controversy about interpretative minutiae that are mainly relevant to the laboratory, not to social life (p. 6)." To help overcome such problems, Boston area universities are developing interdisciplinary courses and programs to prevent lawyers, engineers, and other professionals from being "unfamiliar with the values, attitudes, and methods of other disciplines and unable to synthesize and apply them to social issues (Baram, 1971, p. 538)." An interdisciplinary program titled "Values, Technology, and Society," recently started at Stanford by professors in aeronautical and mechanical engineering, anthropology, chemistry, psychology, etc., provides a variety of courses that examine critical value issues presented by social-technological developments (*Stanford Observer*, 1972).

My position is a search for perspective, not an either-or choice. Assuming a broader and more challenging perspective does not mean we should deny the SET frame of reference. Rather, it assumes that we work to expand and complement it. Given the choice between scientific and non-scientific approaches, I would choose the former (Gage, 1972). However, there are other refined and realistic choices which can be emphasized, such as Weisskopf's (1972), which attempts to relate scientific and technological knowledge and methods within a framework dedicated to the philosophic, social and ethical affairs and concerns of humanity. Also, change can develop through steps, such as suggested by Goodman (1967), to decentralize bureaucratic control and decision-making "to increase the amount of mind and the number of wills initiating and deciding (p. 132)," and "Medieval pluralism," which stresses disputatious and competitive rather than just harmonious relations between concerned interest groups. Hainer's (1968) approach attempts to analyze diverse multicultural behavior in research, development, and engineering and develop a progressive relationship between rationalism, pragmatism, and existentialism with emphasis upon "internal relevance" and social interaction. The distinctions that Tart (1972) makes of observations and theorizations appropriate for varying scientific approaches and concerns, i.e., "state-specific sciences," are also worth consideration.

Although SET approaches should not be discarded, they cannot be perfected to solve their basic limitations. We have become so conditioned to SET advances and defining programs by SET criteria that this may seem heretic to some. However, allowing only such approaches, even with the best intentions and apologies to frame our hopes for what education can become, is to misuse them and inexcusably limit education. Before we rush any further with today's SET processes alone, we ought to consider not only what they are capable of, but what we would like to do for ourselves (Taylor, 1972, pp. 245-266). Tracing psychology's diverse roots and leads, Bakan (1972) argues that psychologists should stop aping the natural sciences by forcing a "fact-module" manipulative approach upon human nature and begin to fulfill its role in the social sciences—"to make man aware of the forces that operate on him (p. 88)." We operate with many implicit assumptions about what is true and good and how they should be affected—all of which may not seem valid in broader and more modest perspective. I would agree with Paul Goodman (1971) that the "chief moral criterion of a philosophic technology is modesty, having a sense of the whole and not obtruding more than a particular function warrants (p. 253)."

A highly touted book by Rivlin (1971), who was an HEW Assistant Secretary for Planning and Evaluation, tends to support the view that SET management procedures are less than infallible and comprehensive, e.g.:

> The cockiness of systems analysts has disappeared with the mystique. If any analyst thought it was going to be easy to make social action programs work better or to make more rational choices among programs, he is by now a sadder and a wiser man. The choices are genuinely hard and the problems are extraordinarily complex and difficult. It is hard to design an income maintenance system that will both assure adequate incomes to the needy and encourage people to work, or a health financing system that will both assure proper care to the sick and encourage efficient use of health resources. It is hard to decide how the government should allocate its resources among different kinds of social action programs. So far the analysts have probably done more to reveal how difficult the problems and choices are than to make the decisions easier (pp. 4-5).

However, although Rivlin reports and projects more problems than success with rational, management approaches, she faithfully believes that they will eventually succeed when they are sophisticated enough. Although she shows fair understanding of how difficult it is to develop adequate performance measures in education and other areas of social services, her suggestions on how to overcome the problem seem vague. For example, she proposes two rules to develop measures: 1) "single measures of social services performance should be avoided" and 2) "performance measures must reflect the difficulty of the problem (pp. 142-143)."

Rivlin's suggestions seem most feasible when she calls for management flexibility and tolerance for variation, such as saying that the most creative teachers are likely to develop and adjust new methods as they proceed, "rejecting elements that seem not to be working and substituting others (p. 115)," suggesting that intensive longitudinal analysis of education be conducted without manipulations to learn more about children, programs, and resources (p. 77), urging that decision-making be decentralized and allowing greater freedom of action and more incentive to achievement and "random innovation" for local managers and staffs (pp. 127-128), and when she calls for greater development of and commitment to systematic experimentation to find out what works and does not work (pp. 91-119).

Although they are intended to produce greater performance gains, such developments are very encouraging, since management planning such as that indicates tolerance to focus more broadly upon behavior and to allow for differences in time, place, and persons. Therefore, some leading system analysts are beginning to show that they recognize diverse and complementary approaches to problem-solving and must consider them somehow. I predict that greater overtures to flexibility and more diverse approaches will soon develop in the educational SET community. We can sense the trend in a recent article on the challenges and hopes of educational technology by the director of USOE's Division of Educational Technology (Grayson, 1972), who wrote:

> There are many difficulties in trying to analyze costs, benefits, and effectiveness in education. Many elements are not quantifiable nor easily measurable, and thus they defy strict quantitative analysis . . . . There is no single definition (to how we provide educational opportunity) . . . . Because a benefit cannot be quantified, however, does not mean that it should be ignored (p. 1217).

Hopefully, such overtures will become more common.

Perspective in Respect to the Teacher-Learner Relationship

Perhaps the crux of the problem has to do with the basic nature of teaching-learning processes that is presumed by the prevailing notion of education. In a 1969 note, Getzels (personal correspondence, and Glass, 1971) said that basic knowledge and research influence education much more significantly in their indirect effects upon general paradigms and conceptions of the human being than when specific classroom practices and variables are directly manipulated. Therefore, the heuristic transfer from the prevailing rational SET frame of reference to education often becomes one of predetermining, predicting, and controlling human behavior. Although imposing material rewards and incentives upon learners and educators to the extent we see in performance contracting may be acceptable in the SET perspective, they are not conducive to the human relations and values perspective. Thus, one would arrive at different conclusions depending upon the perspective in use at a particular time, as it seems in Baldridge's (1972) analysis of the feasibility of organizational change through the human relations vs. the political system perspective.

It may be that our perspectives are more situationally determined and divided than we think, i.e., management, research, and development in the SET frame and social interaction in the human relations frame. Nevertheless, there is no doubting which perspective predominates today. As prescriptions for education become more systematically uniform and vested in technological engineering, somehow teachers' and pupils' roles become increasingly predetermined and learned knowledge becomes more certain, absolute, and impersonal (MacDonald and Wolfson, 1970). As Ferry (1968) put it:

> Our educational purposes have never been very clear. Technication may compel removal of the ambiguities and establishment of straightforward aims. But who will undertake this task? How shall we assure that the result is the betterment of children and not the convenience of machines? Are we really all that crazy about efficiency, or what we are told is efficiency? . . . I am not denying that certain advantages to education are offered by the new technology . . . tonic and toxic technology are here mixed in unknown proportions (pp. 52-53).

We know teachers must be far more competent and professionally committed, but we have devoted more attention to the tools and tailoring of teaching than improving spontaneous and open teaching itself. Perhaps in our frustration with unskilled teachers and the great lag in educational improvement, we somehow never really tried to effect education through the teacher as a real professional person. Yet the teacher must be the key factor. Our emphases upon the teacher as technician and the quantitative rather than the qualitative aspects of teacher preparation clearly inhibit the teaching-learning relationship and professional growth. One way to view the problem of performance contracting is that it falsely assumes that teachers can only be functionaries instead of professional leaders (Nash, 1970).

New theory and systematic planning are needed to bring greater focus upon teacher-learner relations and provide processes that maximize the interaction and options of teachers and learners instead of concentrating solely upon reductionist models that may misrepresent education and regiment teachers and learners (Yee, 1971). As others have tended to suggest (Gage, 1963; MacDonald and Wolfson, 1970; Travers, 1967, pp. 515-517), the conditions for effective learning and teaching are complex and interrelated; overemphasis upon one or several mechanical factors or introducing unnatural conditions, such as material incentives, lowers the meaning of education. Performance contracting belittles the hopes of education by corrupting the teacher-learner relation. It clearly shows the critical need to regard the essential qualitative features of teaching and learning beyond which integrity is lost (e.g., Dewey, 1971).

In another paper (Yee, in press), I discussed the historic and continuing professional disparity between classroom teachers and educational scholars, which has greatly increased in recent times due to a growing lack of common background, involvement, and sympathy. The relationship between them has been characterized by scholastic and administrative authority and dependent classroom practice. If teachers and educational scholars continue to have little in common and relate as poorly as they do today, the greater blame will be the educational scholar's, since he is responsible for the preparation of educational workers. We need to develop a new kind of educational leader who can "spark a great public dialogue about the ends and means of education" (Cremin, 1965, p. 117). Such a scholar-practitioner would be prepared through studies in the behavioral sciences and the humanities of education and would seem to combine many of the strengths already characteristic of leading educational practitioners and scholars.

It seems remarkable that performance contracting became such an inflated educational scheme in about three years. In my view, performance contracting is an educational Titanic that forces those involved in education to take perspective. It helps us realize the limits of scientific-economic-technological approaches and the need to develop and relate complementary and diverse perspectives in education.

C.P. Snow's (1963) *Two Cultures* clearly warned the scientific community and the community of arts and letters about the danger of divided approaches to knowledge and problem-solving, which make all sides ignorant for not communicating. He said we should not be "ignorant of imaginative experience, both in the arts and in science, nor ignorant either of the endowments of applied science, of the remediable suffering of most of [our] fellow humans, and of the responsibilities which, once they are seen, cannot be denied (p. 100)." It is quite ironic to be reminded of Snow's single basis of hope—that changes in education at all levels would make such ignorance less likely. The potential contribution of educational scholars in such endeavors is a humanistic and scientific challenge of rare significance.

References

Atkinson, R.C., & Wilson, H.A. Computer-assisted instruction. *Science*, 1968, *162*, 73-77.

Bakan, D. Psychology can now kick the science habit. *Psychology Today*, 1972, *5*, 26-28 & 86-88.

Baldridge, J.V. Organizational change: The human relations perspective versus the political systems perspectives. *Educational Researcher*, 1972, *1* (2), 4-11 & 15.

Baram, M.S. Social control of science and technology. *Science*, 1971, *172*, 535-539.

Barro, S.M. An approach to developing accountability measures for the public schools. *Phi Delta Kappan*, 1970, *52*, 196-205.

Bartley, R.L. On the limits of rationality. *Wall Street Journal*, September 10, 1971.

Beals, R.L. *Politics of social research: An inquiry into the ethics and responsibilities of social scientists.* Chicago: Aldine, 1969.

Beveridge, W.I.B. *The art of scientific investigation.* New York: Random House, 1957.

Blackburn, T.R. Sensuous-intellectual complementarity in science. *Science*, 1971, *172*, 1003-1007.

Blankenship, L.V. History of a commitment. *Science*, 1971, *173*, 317-318.

Bohr, N. *Essays 1958-1962 on atomic physics and human knowledge.* New York: Interscience, 1963.

Boyer, W.H., & Walsh, P. Are children born unequal? *Saturday Review*, 1968, *51*, 61-63 & 77-79.

Brooks, H. Can science survive in the modern age? *Science,* 1971, *174,* 21-30.

Brooks, H., & Bowers, R. The assessment of technology. *Scientific American,* 1970, *222* (2), 13-21.

Brown, M. (Ed.) *The social responsibility of the scientist.* New York: Free Press, 1971.

Bushnell, D.S. ES '70: A systems approach to educational reform. *Education,* 1971, *70,* 61-67 & 75.

Campbell, D.T. Reforms as experiments. *American Psychologist,* 1969, *24,* 409-429.

Campbell, D.T. Comments on the comment by Shaver and Staines. *American Psychologist,* 1972, *27,* 1964.

Center Magazine. Beyond freedom and dignity? 1972, *5* (2), 33-65.

Cremin, L.O. *The genius of American education.* Pittsburgh: University of Pittsburgh Press, 1965.

Cronbach, L.J., & Suppes, P. (Eds.) *Research for tomorrow's schools: Disciplined inquiry for education.* New York: Macmillan, 1969.

Dewey, J. Democracy and education. In A.H. Yee (Ed.), *Social interaction in educational settings.* Englewood Cliffs, N.J.: Prentice-Hall, 1971, 257.

Educational Researcher. AAAS panel considers role of scientists in policy making, 1972, *1* (2), 17-18.

Ellul, J. *The technological society.* New York: Random House, 1964.

Enthoven, A.C., & Smith, K.W. *How much is enough?* New York: Harper and Row, 1971.

Ferkiss, V.C. *Technological man: The myth and the reality.* New York: Braziller, 1969.

Ferry, W.H. Must we rewrite the Constitution to control technology? *Saturday Review,* 1968, *51* (9), 50-54.

Gage, N.L. Paradigms for research on teaching. In N.L. Gage (Ed.), *Handbook for research on teaching.* Chicago:

Rand McNally, 1963, 94-141.

Gage, N.L. Replies to Shockley, Page, and Jensen: The causes of race difference in I.Q. *Phi Delta Kappan,* 1972, *53,* 422-427.

Gallup, G. The third annual survey of the public's attitudes toward the public schools. *Phi Delta Kappan,* 1971, *53,* 33-48.

Gell-Mann, M. How scientists can really help. *Physics Today,* 1971, *24* (5), 23-25.

Glass, G.V. Educational knowledge use. *Educational Forum,* 1971, *36,* 21-29.

Goodman, P. *Like a conquered province: The moral ambiguity of America.* New York: Random House, 1967.

Goodman, P. Can technology be humane? In M. Brown (Ed.), *The social responsibility of the scientist.* New York: Free Press, 1971, 247-265.

Grayson, L.P. Costs, benefits, effectiveness: Challenge to educational technology. *Science,* 1972, *175,* 1216-1222.

Hainer, R.M. Rationalism, pragmatism, and existentialism. In E. Glatt & M.W. Shelley (Eds.), *The research society.* New York: Gordon & Breach, 1968, 7-50.

Horowitz,I.L. (Ed.). *The use and abuse of social science.* New Brunswick, N.J.: Transaction Books, 1971.

Kelman, H.C. *A time to speak: On human values and social research.* San Francisco: Jossey-Bass, 1968.

Kennedy, W.O., & Vega, M. Negro children's performance on a discrimination task is a function of examiner race and verbal incentive. In A.H. Yee (Ed.), *Social interaction in educational settings.* Englewood Cliffs, N.J.: Prentice-Hall, 1971, 366-372.

Klein, S.P. The uses and limitations of standardized tests in meeting the demands for accountability. *UCLA Evaluation Comment,* 1971, *2* (4), 1-7.

Krantz, D.H. Measurement structures and psychological laws.

Science, 1972, *175,* 1427-1435.

Lehmann, H. The systems approach to education. *Audio-visual Instruction,* 1968, *13,* 144-148.

Lessinger, L. *Every kid a winner: Accountability in education.* New York: Simon and Schuster, 1970.

Logsdon, J.M. *Decision to go to the moon.* Cambridge, Mass.: M.I.T. Press, 1970.

MacDonald, J.B., & Wolfson, B.J. A case against behavioral objectives. *Elementary School Journal,* 1970, *71,* 119-128.

Mandelbaum, L. Apollo: How the United States decided to go to the moon. *Science,* 1969, *163,* 649-654.

Mills, C.W. *The power elite.* New York: Oxford University Press, 1956.

Morison, R.S. Science and social attitudes. *Science,* 1969, *165,* 150-156.

Nash, R.J. Commitment to competency: The new fetishism in teacher education. *Phi Delta Kappan,* 1970, *52,* 240-243.

Nisbet, R. *The degradation of the academic dogma: The university in America, 1945-70.* New York: Basic Books, 1971.

Office of Economic Opportunity. *An experiment in performance contracting: Summary of preliminary results.* Washington, D.C.: OEO Office of Planning, Research, and Evaluation, 1972.

Oppenheimer, J.R. *Science and the common understanding.* New York: Simon and Schuster, 1953.

Oppenheimer, J.R. Analogy in science. *American Psychologist,* 1956, *11,* 127-135.

Popper, K.R. *The logic of scientific discovery.* New York: Harper, 1959.

Rapping, E.A., & Rapping, L.A. Politics and morality in academe. *Saturday Review,* 1968, *51* (42), 64-65 &

75-76.

Rivlin, A.M. *Systematic thinking for social action.* Washington, D.C.: Brookings Institution, 1971.

Saretsky, G. Every kid a hustler. *Phi Delta Kappan,* 1971, *52,* 595-596.

Sattler, J.M. Racial "experimenter effects" in experimentation, testing, interviewing, and psychotherapy. *Psychological Bulletin,* 1970, *73,* 137-160.

Schaeffer, K.H., Fink, J.B., Rappaport, M., Wainstein, L., & Erickson, C.J. *The knowledge analyst: An approach to structuring man-machine systems.* Washington, D.C.: Air Force Office of Scientific Research, Office of Aerospace Research, Technical Report AFOSR, 4490, 1963.

Schon, D.A. *Beyond the stable state.* London: Temple Smith, 1971.

Schorer, M. *Sinclair Lewis: An American life.* New York: Delta, 1961.

Schutz, R.E. Measurement aspects of performance contracting. *NCME Measurement in Education,* 1971, *2* (3), 1-4.

Shaver, P., & Staines, G. Problems facing Campbell's "Experimenting Society." *American Psychologist,* 1972, *27,* 161-163.

Skinner, B.F. *Beyond freedom and dignity.* New York: Alfred A. Knopf, 1971.

Smith, M.B. *Social psychology and human values.* Chicago: Aldine, 1969.

Snow, C.P. *The two cultures and a second look.* Cambridge, Mass.: Cambridge University Press, 1963.

Stake, R.E. Testing hazards in performance contracting. *Phi Delta Kappan,* 1971, *52,* 583-588.

Stanford Observer. Values, technology and values. April 1972, p. 3.

Tart, C.T. States of consciousness and state-specific sciences. *Science,* 1972, *176,* 1203-1210.

Taylor, A.J. Those magnificent men and their teaching machines. *Educational Forum,* 1972, *36,* 245-266.

Thorson, T.L. *Biopolitics.* New York: Holt, Rinehart and Winston, 1970.

Time Magazine, Money-back schools: Unclear balance sheet, October 11, 1971(a), p. 78.

Time Magazine. The particular tragedy of Robert McNamara. July 5, 1971(b), p. 21.

Travers, R.M.W. *Essentials of learning.* (2nd ed.) New York: Macmillan, 1967.

Vallance, T.R. Social science and social policy: Amoral methodology in a matrix of values. *American Psychologist,* 1972, *27,* 107-113.

Ward, T. Curricular accountability through testing. *In using tests in curriculum evaluation.* Ann Arbor, Michigan: Bureau of School Services, University of Michigan, 1970, 3-10.

Weisskopf, V.F. The significance of science. *Science,* 1972, *176,* 138-146.

Yamamoto, K., Jones, J.P., & Ross, M.B. A note on the processing of classroom observation records. *American Educational Research Journal,* 1972, *9,* 29-44.

Yee, A.H. (Ed.) *Social interaction in educational settings.* Englewood Cliffs, N.J.: Prentice-Hall, 1971.

Yee, A.H. Classroom teachers and educational scholars: What do they have in common? In D. Allen (Ed.), *Controversy in education.* Philadelphia: W.B. Saunders, in press.

4

Behavioral Objectives, Performance Contracting, Systems Management and Education

Louis Fischer and Robert Sinclair

The preceding papers of Professors Apple, Popham, and Yee address several significant current issues central to the conduct and improvement of education programs. While the issues are ostensibly those identified in the title, namely, behavioral objectives, performance contracting, and systems management, there is scarcely an area of education unrelated to a thorough treatment of them. Implicit in these three issues are most of the axiological and epistemological problems related to curriculum as well as to conflicting conceptions of the "good society," a concern of social philosophy. Clearly, neither the papers nor this discussion can adequately treat the problems implicit in these broad areas, yet they can serve as stimulants for further professional dialogue and research.

The three papers *represent* very different scholarly positions. Also, the authors *present* divergent intellectual and personal styles by the sources they draw upon, the analogies they use, their choice of language, and the degree of detached reflection or ideological partisanship they exhibit. Neither Apple, Popham, nor Yee can be accused of having "an irrational passion for dispassionate rationality." In other words, their respective commitments are quite clear and they are not fence-sitters.

If objectivity is the highest virtue in a symposium, then Professor Yee receives the gold medal, and Professors Apple and Popham the silver and bronze, in that order. Comments will be made on substantive issues associated with each paper later; as an introductory note we simply indicate that Yee exhibits more of an objective and even-tempered detachment throughout his analysis than his colleagues, who have very thinly veiled biases, if not prejudices. In short, the concerns of Professor Apple are serious and must not be ignored. However, they are more defensible as warnings against probable misuses of systems management approaches than against defects *inherent in* the procedure. There are good grounds for his concerns and warnings; he explicitly recognizes the neutrality of systems thought, yet the clear implication that systems theory in education is inherently defective has not been established. Thus, while Apple's main points are ideologically influenced, he does not make explicit his premises nor does he establish their superiority to alternative premises, which he suggests are necessarily part of systems management approaches to education.

Professor Popham also falls short of the ideal of objectivity; detached reflection or even thorough analysis is what turns out to be almost a sales-pitch for behavioral objectives. His way of posing a global question at the beginning of his paper, "How should we go about promoting improvements in the educational enterprise?" is in itself problematic. He should not be surprised to find it difficult to answer such a question; in fact, what is amazing is that he accepts the question as a meaningful one and then in all seriousness proposes that objective-based management strategies constitute the near-perfect solution. While repeatedly asserting the primacy of rational decision-making, the reliance on evidence, and the consideration of unintended consequences, the paper is not convincing either in its depth of reasoning, presentation and consideration of evidence, or weighing of unintended consequences attendant upon a heavy reliance on behavioral objectives, performance contracting, or systems management. In short, Professor Popham ignores his own stated commitments. Furthermore, on the matter of values as they relate to preferences, selection of educational goals and objectives, he is simply confused.

These general claims concerning the three papers are serious and they might appear more compelling due to the brevity of our statement. With the space limitations imposed upon us, we stand by such general indictments; and the comments that follow will establish their legitimacy as well as raise specific concerns we consider to be central to the future development or demise of systems management approaches to education.

In order to minimize overlap and repetition, the three papers will not be discussed separately. We will refer to ideas in each of the papers as relevant to our discussion. Performance contracting will receive the least explicit attention, since the Yee paper highlighted its major problems and cited excellent sources for readers eager to pursue this development. Furthermore, many of the problems we address related to educational objectives also apply to performance contracting.

Aims, Goals, and Objectives
The persistent debates about the aims, goals, and objectives of education have been with us since recorded history. The following complaint, voiced by Aristotle in 300

B.C., with some modifications in style could be found in current literature:

> There are doubts concerning the business [of education] since all people do not agree in those things which they would have a child taught, both with respect to improvement in virtue and a happy life: nor is it clear whether the object of it should be to improve the reason or rectify the morals. From the present mode of education we cannot determine with certainty to which men incline, whether to instruct a child in what will be useful to him in life, or what tends to virtue, or what is excellent; for all these things have their separate defenders.[1]

In spite of the mounting literature related to this phase of educational efforts, the confusions and disagreements persist. To put it simply, all discussions of aims, goals, and objectives relate to the common-sense question of why we should have schools. Since schools are not natural phenomena but are created by men, some human purposes must justify their creation and perpetuation. Overall aims in turn help us frame goals, which are translated into objectives. Objectives are instrumental to the achieving of goals which were somehow derived from an examination of aims. While the relationships of objectives to goals and to guiding aims is usually agreed upon, consensus shatters as we ask the "so what" question.

Professor Popham explicitly rejects the tradition that begins with general aims and attempts to translate these into instructional objectives and then into learning opportunities.

He places all his faith in behavioral objectives by choosing them from large pools of measurable instructional objectives and thus appears to provide the basic fuel for the powerful educational machine of systems management. Yee raises questions about the current adequacy of measurable objectives, the problems and limitations of quantification, and the shortsightedness of disvaluing non-measurable educational objectives. Our reservations are aimed at Popham's analysis.

While he chides "certain of these systems analysis proponents" for their "almost religious devotion to their methodology," his uncritical acceptance of behavioral objectives and the conscious choice to exclude any serious comment about systems not so based makes one wonder whether he is simply shaking his tambourine for a competing religion. In fact, Popham gives parsimony as his first reason for employing instructional objectives as an organizing rubric and its use by the National Assessment of Educational Progress as the second. Parsimony in communicating information is insufficient to justify the acceptance of behaviorism, and reference to the National Assessment is merely an argument from authority. Incidentally, the use of instructional objectives for the National Assessment is determined by assessment principles for testing human skills and abilities, not by systems management procedures for a large-scale enterprise.[2] Further, the development of instrumentation for the National Assessment does not include deriving criteria for evaluation from large pools of predetermined behavioral objectives. In short, Popham's mention of the National Assessment to support behavioral objectives as the organizing dimension for systems analysis strategy is inappropriate and actually counter to his reasoning on how objectives should be selected. We cannot help but wonder whether the entire model he is advancing is not based on an uncritical acceptance of behaviorism[3] and its focus on measurability on the one hand and the increased governmental funding of programs based on the assumption that all educational outcomes are measurable, on the other. Reference to California's current efforts to appraise its higher education, together with other references to funded projects based on the primacy of measurable objectives, strengthen the latter reservation.

Are Preferences Values?

All three papers recognize the difficulties and conflicts entailed in specifying objectives of schooling. While Apple emphasizes the ideological dimension of curricular objectives, Popham uses a clever method that purports to avoid "value preferences and informal assertions of people." Instead, he says: "We present people with objectives from which they choose those they consider most important." The effort to achieve clarity in stating objectives is laudable, indeed. However, for the sake of clarity let us not equate preferences with values, nor think that we can avoid the value selection difficulties in choosing educational objectives by resorting to clever statistical "needs assessments."

Philosophers commonly distinguish "prizing" from "appraisal," the former being a preference that may or may not be justifiable, while the latter signifies the more complex processes involved in grounding value assertions.[4] We all have personal preferences which, upon careful appraisal, we would like not to have. A preference might be the result of an impulse, uncritical conditioning, or unexamined tradition. By contrast, a value necessarily entails deliberation and the careful analysis of alternatives, their antecedents and consequences, before choosing. Popham's use of objective pools from which groups will indicate their preferences, which then become the objectives of the system, is faulty on several grounds. First, it ignores the distinction between preferences and values and thus ignores values as an important data source for building curriculum.[5] Second, it commits the naturalistic fallacy of implying that we can move from the "is to the ought." That is, by finding out what people prefer now we can assert what they ought to prefer in educational objectives. The scheme for selecting objectives proposed by Popham does not include a viable procedure for moving from what is preferred by a group (preferences made within the parameters of the pool of objectives) to what is desirable. Third, it puts the cart before the horse in insisting that we accept only measurable behaviors as worthwhile in our construction of educational objectives. The more justifiable sequence, and the sequence accepted by general systems theory, begins with aims and goals and uses objectives as instruments to their attainment. Fourth, the selection of objectives from a pool can serve as a means to legitimize already existing practices that are inappropriate. Simply sifting through numerous objectives to discover those that permit one to continue doing exactly what is already going on is one possible use of the pool of objectives. Also, associated with this possibility is the fact that when objectives are simply rated and selected for instruction they often do not affect the classroom performance of the teacher. In other words, the selection of objectives from a pool does not necessarily result in instructional behavior designed to reach preferred objectives. Finally, the mounting popularity of the pool as a method of identifying objectives is in a major way determined by its convenience for presenting surface motions of accountability. One way used to combat the current press for accountability is for anxious educators to display and report the processes or procedures used for *determining* effects rather than to report actual results and the complementing variables that foster such results. The listing, then, of many behavioral objectives often radiates the unfounded notion that a system is on top of their accountability responsibilities when in reality they simply have a list of objectives selected from a pool.

Our comments must not be considered an indictment of behavioral objectives *per se.* Rather, we object to the uncritical acceptance of them and their apparent reverence as the only worthwhile educational pursuit.[6] The exclusive reliance on quantifiable outcomes of education entails both philosophic problems and curriculum dangers. Philosophically, there appears to be a reliance on what has by now become a slogan, namely: "Whatever exists, exists in some quantity; therefore it can be measured." There are, of course, various problems implicit in such a statement. First, how do we assert that whatever exists, exists in some quantity? Why not in some quality, some dimensions of which are quantifiable? There are alternative ontological presuppositions possible in this conflict and they lead to different consequences. To point up at least one further problem with the slogan, the "therefore it can be measured" does not follow *unless* by quantity we imply measurement, in which case the entire statement is a tautology. In the educational environment there exist a variety of relationships among teachers and students as well as students and students. Since they exist, can we say that they exist in some quantity and therefore they can be measured? Furthermore, what justifies the proponent of behavioral objectives in the assertion that those aspects of the relationships which are measurable *ipso facto* are more worthwhile?[7]

What we identify as a key curriculum danger is analogous to Gresham's Law, in that an overemphasis on behavioral objectives will drive out of our schools the various and worthwhile objectives not quantifiable. In outline form the argument proceeds as follows: With the continuing shortage of public funds for the schools, the quest for efficiency and effectiveness will lead to increased efforts to measure the "products" of the schools. Schools, in order to gain support from a public dominated by a business ethic, will support and emphasize those aspects of the curriculum where the outcomes are quantifiable and thus measurable. The non-measurable aspects of the curriculum, what some technical-minded people pejoratively call "mystical," are likely to be shortchanged as a consequence. The intention here is not to suggest that latent aspects of the curriculum cannot be identified or described in a quantifiable form. Rather, the purpose is to suggest that the use of only measurable objectives characterized by criteria of specificity that limit their attention to the most obvious tends to do injustice to variables in the educational environment that are salient yet more hidden.[8]

It is interesting to note, perhaps to remind Professor Popham, who often refers to himself as a pragmatist, that John Dewey, still acknowledged to be the leading pragmatic educational philosopher, while valuing science and mathematics, also proposed that ultimately they are to be handmaidens to the arts and to aesthetic experience. The measurable, while very important for the intelligent control and management of human affairs, is in the final analysis instrumental to aesthetic and thus consummatory experience.

Ends and Means

Professor Apple gives clear warnings of the ideological bias implicit in educational systems management. He repeatedly warns that systems approaches are not neutral analytic means. He recognizes, however, that in principle, systems theory, when used for purposes of illumination, is not inherently biased. In very insightful ways Apple establishes the point that, when used in education, systems approaches tend no longer to be ideologically neutral, but become powerful means transfused with conservative biases. The same allegations concerning the conservatism of systems approaches have been made in other fields as well, for example in the application of systems theory to politics and to law. For example,

Another major limitation to the use of political systems analysis is that description is emphasized to the apparent exclusion of prescription. The stress is on what *is*, and there is a danger that the systems analyst can implicitly use his analysis to defend or maintain the status quo. Thus under the guise of empirical theory, systems analysis can potentially if inadvertently assume a politically conservative posture. Yet systems analysis is not necessarily incompatible with normative consideration of systemic processes and output. Systems analysts simply try to distinguish between norms (what should be) and facts (what is). Perhaps the best way for the systems analyst to avoid the problem is to explicitly articulate policy preferences and the norms (whatever they may be) against which the system is evaluated. Proposals for

reform would then be not simply in the realm of
making the system more efficient (which, of
course, implicitly reflects a conservative value) but
rather shaping the system so that it can better
accomplish those ends and produce those outputs
that the analyst thinks it should.[9]

Granted that systems theory as an analytic tool is
ideologically neutral, it is doubtful that it can remain
unbiased when applied to the value-laden process of schooling. If it can be no more neutral than our schools, can we at
least insure that a variety of value positions are respected in
the system? This would in part relate to the parameters of
the system as well as the various publics which would have a
voice concerning aims, "inputs" of various kinds, as well as
"outputs" and evaluations. What one considers the parameters of the system is crucial. Popham seems to be too
restrictive in his parameters. He seems to consider the
schooling enterprise to be the complete system, not including
the larger encompassing social system that influences the
subsystem of the school. Unless the parameters are more
inclusive, the possibility of the school's using systems analysis
methodology to influence problems like racism, civil rights,
busing, and other social concerns will go begging. Popham's
analysis seems to overlook the issue of ideological bias, but
perhaps he accepts whatever bias results from his proposed
method of deriving objectives through reactions to objectives
pools. His position, however, suffers from a more serious
error, namely, the separation of means and ends. Curriculum
workers throughout history have fallen into this error and it
is against such separation that Dewey spoke:

In other words, the external idea of the aim leads to a separation of means from end, while an end which grows up within an activity as plan for its direction is always both ends and means, the distinction being only one of convenience. Every means is a temporary end until we have attained it. Every end becomes a means of carrying activity further as soon as it is achieved. We call it end when it marks off the future direction of the activity in which we are engaged; means when it marks off the present direction. Every divorce of end from means diminishes by that much the significance of the activity and tends to reduce it to a drudgery from which one would escape if he could . . . .[10]

Dewey's concern about externally imposed ends led to a further warning:

The vice of externally imposed ends has deep roots. Teachers receive them from superior authorities; these authorities accept them from what is current in the community. The teachers impose them upon children. As a first consequence, the intelligence of the teacher is not free; it is confined to receiving the aims laid down from above. Too rarely is the individual teacher so free from the dictation of authoritative supervisor, textbook on methods, prescribed course of study, etc., that he can let his mind come to close quarters with the pupil's mind and the subject matter. This distrust of the teacher's experience is then reflected in lack of confidence in the responses of pupils. The latter receive their aims through a double or treble external imposition, and are constantly confused by the conflict between the aims which are natural to their own experience at the time and those in which they are taught to acquiesce. Until the democratic criterion of the intrinsic significance of every growing experience is recognized, we shall be intellectually confused by the demand for adaptation to external aims.[11]

In this respect perhaps our most serious concern with Popham's position is that he elevates the curriculum technologist to the position of curriculum theorist or philosopher.[12] By contrast, a different conception rings through the call of John Goodlad that we ". . . infuse the means of education with the values we have hitherto espoused in defining the ends."[13]

Related Concerns

While Professor Yee points up some appropriate reservations philosophers of science hold concerning the SET approaches to complex, value-laden human affairs and while Apple expresses the need to refocus on the critical function of science, we must also raise some other concerns.

We are concerned that the drive for efficient management through systems strategies will further centralize educational decision-making. There are powerful dangers in this both for a theory of democracy and for teaching as a profession. Such centralization is particularly dangerous when viewed in light of the elitism implicit in the fourth paragraph of Popham's paper, which centers on the unsatisfactory nature of human decision-making, as well as in his closing sentence, which states in part, "... if the management system lacks total perfection, it will be so close that the learners it serves won't know the difference." Also, we are concerned that Popham's exclusive reliance on behavioral objectives in his proposed systems management approach would violate one of the necessary requisites of an "open system," that of acquiring "negative entropy" to prevent the disorganization or death of the system.[14] The selection of objectives for a system does not mean that there is no cause to respond to the system by redefining or eliminating initial objectives. Too often the energy of a system is spent only on strategies to accomplish designated objectives or measurement of the progress of the system toward stipulated objectives. If objectives are not reached, new strategies are quickly designed with little attention directed to the possibility that the objectives themselves are inappropriate. Objectives are not permanent, they require continuous revision and elimination. Brackenbury supports this temporary nature of objectives by stating, "Human beings generally like to do a task and be done with it. Unfortunately, objectives are much like dishes. If they are used, they require repeated doing and redoing. Since objectives grow out of experience as well as guide experience, they are never set once and for all."[15]

Finally, we have serious reservations about the conception of teaching and learning as well as the conception of what a school is that is implicit in the large-scale use of business management theories and practices. Will there be room for a variety of teaching styles and learning styles? Will the full range of human intelligence be respected and developed? Specificity, clarity, behavioral objectives, quantification, and measurement certainly exemplify intelligent behavior; however, they do not exhaust it. Witness the intelligence exhibited by the works of such diverse individuals as Shakespeare, Gandhi, Langston Hughes, Henry Moore or Muhammed Ali. Will the schools nurture the growth of their intelligence?

While attempting to develop a systems approach to schooling, we might reconsider this brief statement from *Children and Their Primary Schools*:

> . . . A school is not merely a teaching shop; it must transmit values and attitudes. It is a community in which children learn to live first and foremost as children and not as future adults . . . . Children need to be themselves, to live with other children and with grown-ups, to learn from their environment, to enjoy the present, to get ready for the future, to create and to love, to learn to face adversity, to behave responsibly, in a word, to be human beings.[16]

Can we be confident that behavioral objectives-based, performance contracting, system management strategies in education will enhance the growth of human beings?

Notes

1. Book VIII of *The Politics*.
2. For a definition of assessment and a description of testing characteristics of assessment procedures, see Benjamin S. Bloom, "Toward a theory of testing which includes measurement-evaluation-assessment," in M.C.

Wittrock and David Wiley (editors), *The evaluation of instruction: Issues and problems* (New York: Holt, Rinehart and Winston, Inc., 1970).

3. Norman Valcohn, "Behaviorism as a philosophy," in T.W. Warner (editor), *Behaviorism and phenomenology*, Rice University Semi-centennial Publications (University of Chicago Press, 1964).

4. See, for example, John Dewey, *Theory of valuation*, Chicago (University of Chicago Press, 1939).

5. For a description of how values can be central to the building of curriculum, see John I. Goodlad, *Development of a conceptual system for dealing with problems of curriculum and instruction*, U.S. Department of Health, Education and Welfare, Contract No. SAE-8024, Project No. 454, 1966.

6. Some of our best friends are behaviorists.

7. While behaviorism seems to be a relative newcomer in our schools, it is not that new to philosophy nor to folk wisdom. C.K. Ogden and I.A. Richards explored some philosophic problems related to it in *The meaning of meaning* (London: Kegan, Paul, 1923), while the folk saying "Actions speak louder than words" reflects a commitment to some level of behaviorism.

8. For an assessment procedure to measure some dimensions of the educational environment of elementary schools that are not easily transformed into behavioral objectives, see Robert L. Sinclair, "Elementary school educational environment: Toward schools that are responsive to students," *National Elementary Principal*, Vol. XLIX, No. 5, April, 1970.

9. Sheldon Goldman and Thomas P. Jahnige, *The federal courts as a political system* (New York: Harper & Row, 1971) p. 278.

10. John Dewey, *Democracy and Education* (New York:

Macmillan Paperback Edition, 1961), p. 106

11. *Ibid.*, pp. 108-109.
12. For this point it might be well to read "Technocracy's children," Chapter I of Theodore Roszak's *The making of a counter culture* (Garden City, New York: Anchor Books, 1969).
13. John I. Goodlad, "The educational program to 1980 and beyond," *Designing education for the future, No. 2*, Morphet and Ryan (eds.) (New York: Citation Press, 1967).
14. For a development of this idea, see Chapter 2 of Daniel Katz and Robert Kahn, *The social psychology of organizations* (New York: John Wiley and Sons, Inc., 1966).
15. Robert Brackenbury, "Guidelines to help schools formulate and validate objectives," *Rational Planning in Curriculum and Instruction*, National Education Association, Center for the Study of Instruction, 1967, p. 108.
16. *Children and Their Primary Schools: A Report of the Central Advisory Council for Education (England)*, Vol. 1 (London: Her Majesty's Stationery Office, 1967).

5

Epilogue

W. James Popham

As I review the three original papers in this symposium, it is possible to see a fairly clear continuum of support-rejection for systems analysis procedures. At one extreme, I personally find much to commend systems analysis approaches. At the other extreme, Professor Apple is clearly opposed to educational systems analysis procedures, on a number of grounds. Professor Yee seems to occupy a middle position, identifying both positive and negative aspects of such approaches.

In my estimate, this type of disagreement regarding a potentially impact-laden educational management strategy is healthy. I fear Professor Apple takes my mid-sixties facetious remarks too seriously. There are clear benefits from intellectual discord in this important arena. True enough, I think his position is erroneous, but one should be obliged to deal with such criticisms in order to test the viability of one's own stance. Now I would like to turn, briefly, to some of the specifics raised by Professors Yee and Apple.

One of the major problems troubling Professor Apple is the "philosophical naivety and the strikingly deterministic aspect of systems management as it is applied to education." He then refers to systems analysis proponents who demand that instructional designers be able to specify in advance *all* of the potential learning outcomes of a learning experience. Surely this is an excessively ambitious goal for a systems analyst working with human behavior. My suspicion is that most systems analysts would be happy if educators could specify a reasonable proportion of their instructional intentions, recognizing that real life will undoubtedly not permit them to prespecify all such outcomes. By being able to get a handle on part of our intentions, our subsequent decisions regarding the adequacy of an instructional effort will be that much more defensible. By isolating a segment of an educational system's instructional goals in advance, it is both possible to judge the adequacy of those goals (explicit goals of a system which are inferior can be more readily isolated and discarded) as well as evaluate the quality of the instruction according to the subsequent attainment of those goals. True enough, we cannot cover the entire range of outcomes which may occur as a consequence of an instructional sequence. Nonetheless, by having access to data dealing with such goals, we are in a better-informed position to make decisions regarding both the quality of the goals and the degree to which they have been achieved. Is it "philosophically naive" to attempt to secure partial information rather than *none*? Is it "strikingly deterministic" to attempt to rationally identify what we wish to accomplish in our schools and then design or modify the instructional means to achieve such goals?

There is another disturbing theme in Apple's criticism of systems analysis, namely, the imputation that educational systems analysis approaches require goals which are preordained by others. There is, in reality, nothing associated with educational systems analysis approaches which precludes the possibility of having all citizens heavily involved in the selection of the goals for such systems. Clearly, the needs assessment operations which are becoming increasingly popular throughout the fifty states represent an effort to select systems goals democratically. These needs assessment approaches are characterized by efforts to secure counsel regarding goals from learners, citizens, academicians, etc.

One also has the impression that Apple is concerned about the possible manipulation of citizens through systems analysis approaches. I am personally more concerned about manipulation possibilities under our current sparse-information system than under a system where there is greater access to data regarding educational intentions and resulting outcomes. In a system where citizens do not recognize what is going on, there is far greater possibility that the malevolent individual can exploit the enterprise. Where goals are explicitly stated, and the mechanisms for determining those goals are equally clear, the possibility of manipulation is accordingly reduced.

On this same point, there is nothing associated with systems analysis approaches which excludes the possibility of goal modification after initial selection. Merely because an educational system embarks on a program designed to accomplish certain goals, this does not mean that those goals cannot subsequently be deleted or other goals added. Further, the astute systems analyst will not evaluate the quality of the educational enterprise only in terms of the goals that were prespecified, but will attend to the total consequences of the educational system irrespective of the goals. In recent years, systems analysis-oriented educators have been particularly sensitive to the importance of attending to all the outcomes of an educational enterprise, both those which were intended and those which were not.

Professor Apple appears to find "technology" and "scientific" approaches reprehensible. There are apparently some inherent defects in attempts to think explicitly, plan carefully, and synthesize knowledge incrementally until it yields more powerful ways of dealing with problem situations. There is, of course, the possibility that a potent technology can be directed toward the wrong ends, but that is surely no reason not to search for more effective problem solution vehicles. Just because a surgeon's scalpel might be used by a psychopath to commit murder should not deter us from presenting surgeons with the most efficient operating instruments. I find little terror inherent in the terms "technology" or "science."

Professor Apple's final concerns deal with possible alternatives to systems analysis approaches. Apple dismisses the notion that "*a* single substitute" or "*one* alternative" for systems management approaches should be considered. Thus, one assumes, he will propose *several* alternatives. But, as an examination of his paper will confirm, *there are no multiple alternatives proposed. Indeed, there is not even one.* We find Professor Apple, as many critics, retiring to the role of *illuminator* of ideological and epistemological presuppositions. I suppose we have to have these would-be illuminators, but frankly one wishes that a reasonable number of these well-intentioned illuminators would direct their considerable talents *toward actually improving the quality of education.* It is easier to sit back and censure than to do something constructive. Until these illuminators come up with some appealing, testable alternatives, I shall be wary of their illuminations.

Professor Yee, I believe, strikes the proper note when he

urges systems analysis proponents to be modest in their expectations. The technology of systems analysis, as embryonic as it is, is laden with pitfalls. Excessive claims for the educational raptures to be yielded by systems analytic efforts are surely destined for repudiation.

As Professor Yee also points out, perhaps the most important purpose of systems analysis is to identify the ultimately intuitive elements which generally undergird an ostensibly rational, data-laden system. Clearly, since human beings will be operating these systems analysis procedures, there will be all sorts of human judgment involved in the systems—as well as all sorts of human errors. Systems analysis enthusiasts, the current writer included, have to be reminded by the sage counsel of people such as Professor Yee that the current technology of systems analysis, as well as that to be foreseen in the relatively near future, is far from perfection.

This is an era when the controversy of the sixties regarding the merits of measurable instructional objectives and rigorous educational assessment should be subsiding. We should be listening to each other, not in the role of adversaries, but as constructive critics. I believe that the dialogue initiated by Professors Apple, Yee, and myself may prove helpful along those lines. I ask all of us, however, to avoid straw-man arguments. There are extremists who advocate outrageous positions with respect to systems analysis schemes. These individuals should be thoroughly chastised. Nonetheless, their imprudence should not be used as an excuse to criticize the entire effort to set education on a more rational base.

6

Models of Rationality
and Systems Approaches:
Further Comments

Michael W. Apple

As the reader has no doubt noted, topics such as the one this set of papers has addressed stimulate a good deal of conflict over the conceptual and practical orientations different groups of educators share. Argumentation of this sort is immensely important if education is to proceed to a more sophisticated understanding of the complexity of the problems it faces. All too often proponents of disparate positions talk by each other. They usually limit their intellectual controversies to co-members of their own "invisible colleges." The result has been a peculiar kind of inbreeding in which accepted schools of thought remain unchallenged and past errors are repeated with depressing regularity.

If one of the purposes of this symposium was to begin to rectify this state of affairs and to open up areas of consensus and disagreement among its participants, it has succeeded admirably. As is clear from the papers, Professors Yee and Popham and myself tend to share a sense of the necessity for changing what goes on in schools and, perhaps, even the very nature of these schools themselves. What is also clear is the fact that each of us tends to see with different lenses against a different horizon of assumptions. Since

Professor Popham chose mainly to respond to my paper in his closing comments, most of my comments will be made in relation to his own. This is not, of course, to deny the generally insightful treatment Professor Yee gives to his topic of concern.

Professor Popham states that I am obviously totally against "technology" and "science." The paper makes no such case. What I have argued is that we have been using rather limited views of science, ones that may be conceptually and practically too simple. This problem is compounded by the fact that we have been so overwhelmingly ameliorative in our orientation that there has evolved a strong tendency to deny the utter import of critical self-reflection.

Let me expand this point here and sketch out possibilities for future research. Educators have assumed that there is one model of science and rationality to which it is appropriate to turn. This is *not* the case. The work of Jurgen Habermas, the Frankfurt sociologist and social theorist, is critically important in this regard. He identifies three analytically distinct types of scientific activity, each of which can be used to couch research questions and design institutions.[1] He distinguishes them according to their prevailing interest. First there are the "strict sciences," such as physics and the positivistic social sciences that accept it as a model upon which to pattern themselves. A good example might be a strictly behavioristic psychology. Their dominant interest lies in enhancing technical control and certainty, a fact I mentioned in the body of my article. A significant part of curriculum and educational thought and institutions rests upon this form of rationality.

Second, there are what Habermas calls the "hermeneutic sciences," such as ethnomethodology, symbolic interactionism, psychoanalysis, and, often, certain styles of historiography. The dominant interest here is in human understanding. The "affective" education and sensitivity movements may be a response to the lack of this constitutive interest in our technical common-sense thought about schooling and educational institutions. Finally, there are the "critical sciences," such as critical sociology. The "critical" refers to a continuous attempt to bring presuppositions to a level of awareness and is based upon a dialectical form of logic that is less accepting of the dominant forms of rationality than the other types of scientific activity. The interest here is in the possible reconstruction of institutions so that barriers to human understanding can be removed and political and ethical dialogue can evolve.[2] In so doing, it aims at the emancipation of individuals from supposed "natural" laws of psychology and sociology.

Obviously this is rather abstract. However, we are beginning to see the evolution of critical sciences in the work of such scholars as Alvin Gouldner[3] in the United States, Habermas in Germany, and in the later work of Sartre[4] in France. All are concerned with the increasing tendency in industrialized societies to limit one's forms of thought to those which severely curtail man's capacity for critical self- and social reflection and reconstruction, and which tend to create and legitimate institutions that are relatively unresponsive to human sentiment. A significant aspect of their analysis has been the examination of the process by which technical rules of instrumental action (process/product reasoning, for example) have tended to erode individuals' symbolic ties to each other and have replaced them with only use-value relationships. Such basic investigations may prove much more fruitful in the long run than the understandable but limiting call for immediate payoff.

Professor Popham also argues in his epilogue that it is easier "to sit back and censure than to do something constructive." I would like to make two somewhat different responses to this comment. What seems to be meant is that "if you do not agree with what I am doing, or find conceptual, political, and very practical problems with my procedures, then don't say anything." That is, the ability to stand back and look closely at what we are doing is *not* constructive and is not a necessary ingredient in the process by which all of us can engage in creating responsive educational institutions. While I do not doubt Professor Popham's intense commitment toward improving schools (something I very much share), I do feel it is both historically and programmatically erroneous to use only the present situation to evaluate contributions. If this had been the case in the physical sciences, for instance, one can only guess the abysmal state those fields would be in now.

A second point should be made here. Education is inherently a valuative enterprise. Its body of information is encased in slogan systems,[5] be they those involving the social reconstructionist movement of the thirties and forties, the curriculum reform movement of the past decade, or the current social utility emphasis of systems management. As such, it is imperative that we become aware of the latent commitments and tendencies in our work. Without this awareness, not only do we merely allow values to work through us unconsciously, but we are not fulfilling the rigors required of any form of rational investigation. Education has persistently shied away from such rigor, much to the detriment of the field. The notion of rational investigation leads us to another point of contention.

One topic continually arises in Professor Popham's discussion—that is, a concern for increasing the rationality of educational planning. Professors Yee and Popham and myself share this concern. There does seem to be some serious disagreement over what is implied by the very concept of rationality, however. While Professor Popham tends to limit increasing rationality to becoming more efficient, and while there certainly is a need for this in quite a few aspects of schooling, I would like to argue that education as a field has been primarily concerned with this for nearly all of this century[6] to the exclusion of other important concerns. I would also take the position that this is only a *partial* perspective on rationality. There are a number of forms of rationality besides the process/product modes that dominate education today. As I tried to indicate in the latter portion of my paper, we continue to neglect areas, such as ethical argumentation, which may provide just as much or perhaps even more in the way of crucial tools for designing better educational institutions.

Huebner,[7] for example, discusses five modes of rationality which may be used to evaluate educational encounters—technological (efficiency or process/product), scientific, aesthetic, ethical, and political. Each of these is but a partial perspective on the problem of valuing our activity. The use of any one form in continued isolation from the corrective power of the others can lead to a good deal of difficulty. Systems management procedures as they have been articulated and practiced in education have tended to ignore many of the very real political and ethical problems that we are constantly called upon to deal with in the day-to-day life of education. One can "increase rationality," thus, by broadening the dimensions of the forms of rationality one looks to for support and insight.

Furthermore, anyone familiar with the results of the use of systems management procedures in the operationalization of the systems-oriented models of elementary teacher education developed at ten major sites throughout the country has been made well aware of the institutional rigidity and overemphasis on triviality that has too often evolved.[8] While this is not an "in principle" argument against such approaches, one is strongly tempted to reply to advocates of systems management to give much stronger evidence for its efficacy than has heretofore been the case. One thing educators should have internalized by now is that change is not necessarily progress.

Perhaps the issues surrounding the use of systems management procedures have been clarified just a bit by this dialogue among the symposium participants. At the least, a number of the major aspects have been opened up for the further give-and-take which must follow. We cannot really expect total clarity in our activity or in our planning, however, for education is an ambiguous, exceptionally complex, and even mysterious enterprise. Wittgenstein was rather insightful in his comment that "Whereof one cannot speak, thereof one must remain silent."[9] That is, the inexpressible—that which is really important—cannot be said by discursive means using models appropriated from the natural sciences. It can only be shown in other ways, through nondiscursive forms such as art, literature, and perhaps religious metaphors.[10] The attempt to make all of education "rational" must not ignore this insight.

Notes

1. Jurgen Habermas, *Knowledge and human interests* (Boston: Beacon Press, 1971). See also Michael W. Apple, "Scientific interests and the nature of educational institutions," a paper presented at the American Educational Research Association, Chicago, Illinois, April 4, 1972.
2. Jurgen Habermas, "Toward a theory of communicative competence," *Recent Sociology 2*, Hans Peter Dreitzel, editor (New York: Macmillan, 1970), pp. 114-148.
3. Alvin W. Gouldner. *The coming crisis of western sociology* (New York: Basic Books, 1970).
4. Jean-Paul Sartre, *Search for a method* (New York: Random House, 1963).
5. Paul Komisar and James McClellan, "The logic of slogans," *Language and concepts in education*, B. Othanel Smith and Robert Ennis, editors (Chicago: Rand McNally, 1961), pp. 195-215.
6. Herbert M. Kliebard, "Bureaucracy and curriculum theory," in *Freedom, bureaucracy, and schooling*, Vernon Haubrich, editor (Washington, D.C.: Association for Supervision and Curriculum Development, 1971), pp. 77-93.
7. Dwayne Huebner, "Curricular language and classroom meaning," in *Language and meaning*, James B. MacDonald and Robert R. Leeper, editors (Washington, D.C.: Association for Supervision and Curriculum Development, 1966), pp. 8-26.
8. Even individuals such as Professor Charles E. Johnson, the project director of the Georgia Systems Model of Elementary Teacher Education and a strong advocate of systems management procedures, has been quite disappointed by the practical results of the use of systems

management in conjunction with competency based teacher education programs. Comments made at a Teacher Corps Associates Symposium, New Orleans, June 23, 1972.

9. K.T. Fann, *Wittgenstein's conception of philosophy* (Berkeley: University of California Press, 1971), pp. 31-32.

10. *Ibid.*, pp. 32-33.

7

Feedback

Albert H. Yee

The favorable response of the other writers to my paper is reassuring indeed and prompts me to forego a closing statement. However, I cannot resist the editorial prerogative and will hazard a brief concluding note. The symposium has been an exciting and challenging experience, ever since it was conceived, and through the writings and phone calls that developed after the other participants were invited and agreed to join in this year-long project. Social interaction such as this symposium should be a continuous process; so I chose the concept of feedback for the title of this piece.

My primary orientation to social interaction in education causes me to focus upon teaching and learning activities directly, and not as an aside or implication.* The factors operating in educational settings are multitudinous indeed, but the only ones that can stand educationally irreducible and intact without any others are teachers *and* learners. We have become so involved in the betterment of all and separate factors that we often neglect these obvious key elements of schools. The shotgun approach to educational R & D

---

*Yee, A.H. (Ed.) *Social interaction in educational settings.* Englewood Cliffs, N.J.: Prentice-Hall, 1971.

distributes energy equally around a point but assumes that the various factors are fairly equal in potency. We also take up segmented and tangential viewpoints, as we must at times, but we often overlook the need to relate them very well to some comprehensive and hierarchical framework which focuses explicitly upon the key elements of teaching-learning relations.

Whether one tends to view education from an abstract, philosophical stance as Apple does or from Popham's down-to-earth, pragmatic position, the question remains: What does it mean in terms of the interaction and relations of teachers and learners? How would actualization of the proposals and critiques change and influence classrooms and school systems? I wish that the other writers had given specific critique to my particular orientation as my paper emphasized it, particularly in the last section. I assume that they do agree.

I sympathize with each of the other writers, though I lean more toward the viewpoints expressed by Apple and Fischer and Sinclair. Such a majority was not arranged *a priori*. However, knowing Popham's other recent writings,* I want to empathize with his important concerns and respect his own search for perspective. Hopefully, more pragmatists and educational workers of all persuasions will follow the example. The extensive list of suggested readings that Jay Shores provides in the next chapter might help readers shape and enlarge their own perspective. At least, such a list might cause others to be reflective, as we became, about their

*Popham, W.J. "Objectives '72." *Phi Delta Kappan*, 1972, *53*, 432-435; and Popham, W.J. "Must all objectives be behavioral?" *Educational Leadership*, 1972, *29*, 605-608.

command of the relevant literature, the possible misapplications of management systems approaches in education through superficial knowledge, and how they might be related better to teaching-learning functions. Taking perspective, i.e., seeking varying sources and approaches and viewing them as to their relative importance in developing an integrated whole, should become a greater feature of professional education.

The need for perspective also concerns the proper relationship and communication between the respective roles of leader and practitioner in determining and carrying out school programs and methods. There remains far more promise than fulfillment yet that the value of conceptual or empirical research and development will benefit education and, thereby, society, in fundamental ways. At the present time, the quality and quantity of ideas and facts emanating from academic centers and publications present a force for change that is largely backlogged on shelves and in advanced seminars. What one finds being implemented in schools by teachers and principals seems far behind last year's R & D production; and given the present decision-making process, it is not simply their fault. The changes in schools are often translations in futility; many are innovative in name alone (e.g., modes of team teaching) and superficial, contradictory representations of a concept (e.g., "creativity" and "disadvantaged"). They indicate the need for greater cooperation and common understanding, but educational leaders seem to be developing greater distance between themselves and classroom teachers. While the preparation and characteristics of practitioners remain fairly stable, educational researchers and leaders have progressed considerably in background, qualifications, and role-expectations. The responsibility for developing greater cooperation and relations must be assumed by the educational leadership through steps such as administrative decentralization, promoting closer contact between laboratory and field, forming new leadership roles for practitioners, and revolutionizing teacher preparation.

The search for educational progress and fulfillment through only scientific-economic-technological or tautological frames of reference will continue to be fruitless and arrogant. The nature of education comprises values, needs, and diversities of persons and approaches that will always be greater than any set of fact-modules and philosophical premises one can derive. As I attempted to state in my earlier chapter, I believe the most feasible approach to take in education is a tolerance for and continuous dialogue between contrasting relevant views, seeking viable means that are congruous with broadly defined but clear and humane ends.

I conclude by calling for greater interaction among professional educators, for "the locus of change lies in the interaction of people with people. The greatest and most lasting changes in institutions, as well as in human relations and attitudes, are products of interaction in social movement."* To promote educational progress, practitioners and leaders must learn to communicate more effectively, respond with less self-righteousness, and seek open critique as a rule. Perhaps one of the greatest shortcomings in professional education today is the tendency of educators at all levels to avoid contact with various conceptual and methodological views if they wish, and if in contact, to talk past one another without constructive resolution and commitment. Unfortu-

*Sherif, M. "On the relevance of social psychology." *American Psychologist*, 1970, *25*, 144-156.

nately, insightful concern for students does not always reflect good concern for one's colleagues and contrasting professional views. If educators related to students as they did to each other, schools would be far worse than they are today.

Education is assumed to be a public and community process, but too much of its actual rationale and practice remain private and privileged and, therefore, unevaluated and unchallenged. That is what has happened in modern education, ironically in the name of scientific rigor, economic efficiency, and technical time-savers—and what has occurred in the past under the banner of ephemeral verbal slogans.

Neither is education uninvolved in social-psychological concerns, but it is often forgotten that educational processes and operations concern real people and everyday social settings. If this symposium exhibits any merit at all, I would want it to indicate the value of interchanging viewpoints and approaches toward perspective and the need for improved communication and reflection.

8

A Guide to
Selected Readings in
the Emerging Systems Sciences

Jay H. Shores *

The basis for and operations of education systems management come mainly from general systems theory and from a wide variety of other systems sciences. This adoption of frames of reference from other sources by the field of education has resulted in conceptual associations with diverse disciplinary areas that are typically segmented in relation to reality. Thus, a scholar attempting to examine systems thought and its influence on education may be led to believe that cybernetic, analogical modeling is systems application. However, upon examining another body of literature, he may surmise that operations research is systems application, or that any number of other seemingly diverse areas are systems application. This bibliography is designed to assist those interested in pursuing systems thought in education by providing a tentative categorical list of some of the more cogent literature in the field.

Ludwig von Bertalanffy (1968) provided an excellent history and development of "general system theory." The ideas behind the systems approach are seen as reaching back

*The author thanks Professor Albert H. Yee for suggesting this project and providing assistance in its development.

117

through time to the works of such men as Leibniz, Marx, Hegel, Nicholas of Cusa, Kohler, and Lotka. The advent of current systems philosophy rests with the work of members of the Society for General Systems Research, organized in 1954. The members of this small society initially included the economist, K. Boulding; the biomathematician, A. Rapoport; the physiologist, Ralph Gerard; and the biologist, von Bertalanffy. Such researchers have developed a philosophy of general systems theory that is presented in annual volumes edited by von Bertalanffy and Rapoport entitled *General Systems,* which date from 1956 through the present. The work of the members of this society comprises the stabilizing core of the systems theory field. While not all of the work in systems theory began with these men, they have taken pains to incorporate into their work that of many previous authors.

The general system philosophy of von Bertalanffy, his contemporaries, and interpreters provides a highly useful conceptual framework for the study and development of systems. With their frame of reference, it is possible to visualize the myriad of systems applications as logical outgrowths of a unified conceptual field as it has been shaped to meet the needs of more traditional disciplines. In mathematics, biology, physics, and even in less abstract and precise sciences such as sociology, the effect of the major precepts of general systems theory may be seen in specific application of systems principles. For example, the concept of feedback in physiology was originally associated with the concept *homeostat.* The use of the general systems concept of *feedback* has allowed the depiction of explicit relationships between sets of wider and more complex operations within the physiological being. These conceptions have led to the development of new mathematical models for the biological sciences which undergird the "new" agrobiology. Similar examples to account for information theory, the organismic revolution, game theory, operations research, and other manifestations of the systems approach are readily found. However, the purpose of this bibliographical commentary is not their delineation.

That general systems theory is being utilized by the sciences is obvious. Not so obvious is the fact that the fundamental precepts of general systems have seldom been explicitly related to traditional disciplines. A few truly hybrid disciplines, which may be thought of as systems sciences, have developed within the traditional fields. However, it would appear that most sciences use the systems science of cybernetics as a model to explicate and analyze their own parochial structural developments. Since it should be possible to apply cybernetic principles wherever an area can develop a mathematical algorithm, it is logical to apply cybernetics to these instances. However, such usage may negate or neglect some of the most obvious powers of general systems theory. General systems theory can give a discipline the ability to make comparisons among the many varied living systems which exist in our psycho-physical world to determine the existence of similarities and differences therein. The common application of cybernetic principles limits such comparisons to statements of purely mathematical relationships, to the neglect of other possible structural relationships.

The following selected bibliography is presented as a list of suggested topical readings, which may be used to initiate a study of systems. This classification of the texts and articles is by no means exhaustive or exclusive. A text such as that edited by Bushnell and Allen (1967), is reported under "computer-based instructional systems," because its dominant focus is computers. This particular text also carries articles on systems applications in instruction and systems applications in business education; thus, it could properly fall in each of those categories.

    The writings are compiled in five topical areas. The areas are:

1. *General Systems Theory.* The authors of these writings define general systems and establish the properties of a systems science.

2. *The Systems Approach and Human Behavior.* These writings address themselves to psychological, political, and sociological applications of systems theory exclusive of the educational applications which follow.

   2a. *The Systems Approach in Education.* Relate basic systems ideas to many topics in the field of education.

   2b. *Systems Applications in Instruction.* Describe attempts to apply the systems approach to actual problems of instruction.

   2c. *Computer-based Instructional Systems.* Center upon those instructional applications of systems which have attempted to use the management capabilities of computers. The emphasis of these writings is upon the technical operations of their systems and their possible interrelationships.

   2d. *Systems Application in Educational Administration.* Deal with organizational and planning problems to which concepts of systems have been applied.

3. *Systems Applications in Other Fields.* These writings present problems in other areas of study, mainly biology, physics, and medicine, to which the systems approach has been applied. Writings which present cybernetics as a systems science and focus upon using the systems approach in research are included.

4. *Futuristic Viewpoints.* The authors of these writings project the theories and trends of the systems sciences and other fields into the future.

5. *Perspective Viewpoints.* These are critical writings which focus upon the relationship among man, machine, and the systems approach in contemporary society.

General Systems Theory

Bertalanffy, L. von. An outline of general systems theory. *British Journal of Philosophy and Science,* 1950, *1,* 139-164.

Bertalanffy, L. von. *Robots, men and minds.* New York: Braziller, 1967.

Bertalanffy, L. von. *General systems theory.* New York: Braziller, 1968.

Bertalanffy, L. von, Hempel, C.G., Bass, R.E., and Jonas, H. General system theory: A new approach to unity of science. *Human Biology,* 1951, *23,* 302-361.

Bertalanffy, L. von, and Rapoport, A. (Eds.) *General systems.* Bedford, Mass.: P.O. Box 228, Society for General Systems Research, yearly vols. since 1956.

Boulding, K.E. General systems theory—The skeleton of science. *Management Science,* 1956, *2,* 197-208.

Foerster, H. von, and Zopf, G.W., Jr. (Eds.) *Principles of self-organization.* New York: Pergamon, 1962.

Gray, W., Rizzo, N.D., and Duhl, F.D. (Eds.) *General systems theory and psychiatry.* Boston: Little, Brown, 1968.

Klir, G.J. *An approach to general systems theory.* Princeton: Van Nostrand, 1968.

Mesarovic, M.D. *View on general systems theory.* New York: Wiley, 1964.

Mesarovic, M.D. *Systems theory: Proceedings of a symposium on.* Brooklyn: Polytechnic Institute, 1965.

Mesarovic, M.D. *Systems theory and biology.* New York: Springer-Verlag, 1968.

Murray, M.F. *The thought of Teilhard de Chardin.* New York: Seabury Press, 1966.

Shaw, L. System theory. *Science,* 1965, *149,* 1005.

The Systems Approach and Human Behavior

Allport, G.W. The open system in personality theory. *Journal of Abnormal and Social Psychology,* 1960, *61,* 301-310.

Attneave, F. *Application of information theory to psychology.* New York: Holt, Rinehart and Winston, 1959.

Buckley, W. *Sociology and modern systems theory.* Englewood Cliffs, N.J.: Prentice-Hall, 1967.

Carter, L.J. Systems approach: Political interest rises. *Science,* 1966, *153,* 1222-1224.

Gagné, R.M. (Ed.) *Psychological principles in system development.* New York: Holt, Rinehart and Winston, 1965.

Goldman, S., and Jahnige, T.P. *The federal courts as a political system.* New York: Harper and Row, 1971.

Grinker, R.R. (Ed.) *Toward a unified theory of human behavior.* New York: Basic, 1967.

Grodius, F.S. *Control theory and biological systems.* New

York, Columbia University, 1963.

Hall, A.D. *A methodology for systems engineering.* Princeton: Van Nostrand, 1962.

Hoggatt, A.C., and Balderston, F.E. (Eds.) *Symposium on simulation models: Methodology and applications to the behavioral sciences.* Cincinnati: South-Western, 1964.

Kalmus, H. (Ed.) *Regulation and control in living systems.* New York: Wiley, 1966.

Kleinmuntz, B. (Ed.) *Concepts and the structure of memory.* New York: Wiley, 1967.

Lindsy, D.B., and Lumsdaine, A.A. (Eds.) *Brain function and learning: Proceedings of the Fourth Conference on Brain Function—UCLA Forum in Medical Sciences.* Los Angeles: University of California Press, 1967.

Loehlin, J.C. *Computer models of personality.* New York: Random House, 1968.

Meadows, P. Models, systems, and science. *American Sociological Review,* 1957, *22,* 3-9.

Miller, J.G. Towards a general theory for the behavioral sciences. *American Psychologist,* 1955, *10,* 513-531.

Miller, N. Comments on theoretical models. *Journal of Personality,* 1951, *20,* 82-100.

Parsons, T. *The social system.* New York: Free Press, 1957.

Porter, W.A. *Modern foundations of systems engineering.* New York: Macmillan, 1966.

Rivlin, A.M. *Systematic thinking for social action.* Washington, D.C.: Brookings Institution, 1971.

Rogers, C.R., and Skinner, B.F. Some issues concerning the control of human behavior. *Science,* 1956, *124,* 1057-1066.

Schaeffer, K.H., Fink, J.B., Rappaport, M., Wainstein, L., and Erickson, C.J. *The knowledgeable analyst: An approach to structuring man-machine systems.* Washington, D.C.: Air Force Office of Scientific Research, Office of

Aerospace Research, Technical Report AFOSR 4490, 1963.

Simon, H.A. *Models of man.* New York: Wiley, 1957.

Simon, H.A. Do machines operate the way people do? *Technological Review,* 1961, *63,* 20.

Simon, H.A. A note on mathematical models for learning. *Psychometrika,* 1962, *27,* 417-418.

Simon, H.A. An information processing theory of intellectual development. In C. Kuhlman and W. Kessen (Eds.). *Thought in the young child. Monographs of the society for research in child development,* 27 (2), 150-161. Yellow Springs, Ohio: Antioch Press, 1962.

Simon, H.A. Computer simulation of human thinking and problem solving. In M. Greenberger (Ed.), *Management and the computer of the future.* New York: Wiley, 1962, 94-133.

Simon, H.A., and Clarkson, G.P.E. Simulation of individual and group behavior. *American Economic Review,* 1960, *50,* 920-932.

Simon, H.A., and Feigenbaum, E.A. An information processing theory of some effects of similarity, familiarization, and meaningfulness in verbal learning. *Journal of Verbal Learning and Verbal Behavior,* 1964, *3,* 385-396.

Simon, H.A., and Gregg, L.W. Process models and scholastic theories of simple concept formation. *Journal of Mathematical Psychology,* 1967, *4,* 246-276.

Simon, H.A., and Newell, A. Computer simulation of human thinking. *Science,* 1961, *134,* 2011-2017.

Simon, H.A., and Newell, A. Information processing in computer and man. *American Scientist,* 1964, *52,* 281-300.

Simon, H.A., and Newell, A. Simulation of human processing of information. *American Mathematical Monthly,* 1965, *72,* 2, Part II, Computers and Computing, 111-118.

Snyder, H.I. *Contemporary educational psychology: Some models applied to the school setting.* New York: Wiley, 1968.

Stagner, R. Homeostasis as a unifying concept in personality theory. *Psychological Review,* 1951, *58,* 5-17.

Wathen-Dunn, W. (Ed.) *Models for the perception of speech and visual form.* Cambridge, Mass.: The Massachusetts Institute of Technology Press, 1967.

The Systems Approach in Education

Adelson, M. System approach: A perspective. *Wilson Library Bulletin,* 1968, *42,* 711-715.

Anderson, G.E., Jr. Are you ready to learn how operations analysis works? *Nation's Schools,* 1968, *81,* 96.

Arnold, M. *Vocational technical and continuing education in Pennsylvania: A systems approach to state-local program planning.* Pennsylvania: Department of Public Instruction, 1969.

Arnstein, G.E. Schoolmen: Don't boggle at the systems concept; you've probably been using it by a different name. *Nations Schools,* 1967, *80,* 76-77.

Banathy, B.H. The systems approach. *Modern Language Journal,* 1967, *51,* 281-289.

Barson, J. Standard operating procedures for a learning resources center: A system for producing systems. *Audiovisual Instruction,* 1965, *10,* 278-379.

Barson, J., and Heinrich, R. Systems approach. *Audiovisual Instruction,* 1966, *11,* 431-433.

Bern, H.A. Wanted: Educational engineers. *Phi Delta Kappan,* 1967, *48,* 230-236.

Bern, H.A., *et al.* Reply to questions about systems. *Audiovisual Instruction,* 1965, *10,* 366-370.

Bishop, L.S. Systems concept. *Educational Leadership,* 1967, *24,* 676.

Bishop, L.S., *et al.* Supervisor and curriculum director at work: Systems approach to information flow and decision making. *Association for Supervision and Curriculum Development Yearbook,* 1965, 127-128.

Blaschke, C.L. DOD: Catalyst in educational technology. *Phi Delta Kappan,* 1967, *48,* 208-214.

Bode, H.F., Mosteller, F., Tukey, F., and Winsor, C. The education of a scientific generalist. *Science,* 1949, *109,* 553.

Bouley, P.C. Tonic or toxic? Systems analysis. *Arizona Teacher,* 1969, *57,* 6-9.

Bushnell, D.S. ES '70: A systems approach to educational reform. *Education,* 1971, *70,* 61-67 & 75.

Churchman, C.W. On the design of educational systems. *Audiovisual Instruction,* 1965, *10,* 361-365.

Clark, E.M. Systems approach: What it is and how it applies to elementary education. *Instructor,* 1966, *76,* 74.

Cogswell, J.F. Systems analysis and computer simulation in the implementation of media. *Audiovisual Instruction,* 1965, *10* (5), 384-386.

Cohodes, A. Using the systems approach is easier than defining it. *Nations Schools,* 1968, *82,* 16.

Cook, D.L. The impact of systems analysis on education. Paper presented at Seminar on Systems Analysis, Temple University, Philadelphia, Pennsylvania, April 18, 1968.

Decker, E.H. Systems approach: A new educational technique. *Science Teacher,* 1968, *35,* 26-27.

DeSimone, D.V. (Ed.) *Education for innovation.* New York: Pergamon, 1968.

Egbert, R.L., and Cogswell, J.F. *System design for a continuous progress school: Part 1.* Santa Monica,

Calif.: System Development Corp., 1964a.

Egbert, R.L., and Cogswell, J.F. *System design for a continuous progress school: Part 2—Surveillance and detection system.* Santa Monica, Calif.: System Development Corp., 1964b.

Eisele, J.E. The computer as a tool for curriculum development and instructional management. A paper presented to the annual conference of the American Psychological Association, March, 1970.

Engler, D. All right computer, explain systems approach. *Nations Schools,* 1967, *80,* 57-59.

Entwisle, D.R., and Convisor, R. Input-output analysis in education. *High School Journal,* 1969, *52,* 192-198.

Eraut, M.R. Instructional systems approach to course development. *Audiovisual Communications Review,* 1967, *15,* 91-101.

Freedman, M. Toward a science of educational communications. *Audiovisual Instruction,* 1969, *14,* 112.

Gagné, R.M. Learning hierarchies. Presidential Address, Division 15, American Psychological Association. Berkeley, August 31, 1968.

Glaspey, J.L. Can modern management techniques be applied to education? *Association of School Business Officials U.S. and Canada Proc.,* 1967, *53,* 254-265.

Goldberg, A.L. First steps in the systems approach. *Audiovisual Instruction,* 1965, *10,* 382-383.

Gordon, P.J. All very well in practice! But how does it work out in theory? *Wilson Library Bulletin,* 1968, *42,* 676-685.

Hartley, H.J. Twelve hurdles to clear before you take on systems analysis. *American School Board Journal,* 1968, *156,* 16-18.

Homme, L., C'deBaca, P., Cottingham, L., and Homme, A. What behavioral engineering is. *Psychological Record,*

1968, *18*, 425.

Hurwitz, F.L. What kind of a design? *Adult Leadership,* 1968, *17*, 55-56.

Joyce, B. Principal and his staff: The multiple systems approach to curriculum. *National Elementary Principal,* 1968, *48*, 24-29.

Joyce, B.R. *Man, medium, machine.* Washington: NEA, 1967.

Kaufman, R.A. System approach to education: Derivation and definition. *Audiovisual Communications Review,* 1968, *16*, 415-425.

Kershaw, J.A., and McKean, R.N. Systems analysis and education. Research memorandum of the Rand Corporation, Santa Monica, Calif., 1959.

Kong, S.L. Education in the cybernetic age: A model. *Phi Delta Kappan,* 1967, *49*, 71-74.

Kristy, N.F. Future of educational technology. *Phi Delta Kappan,* 1967, *48*, 240-243.

Lave, R.E., Jr. and Kyle, D.W. Application of systems analysis to educational planning. *Comparative Education Review,* 1968, *12*, 39-56.

Lehman, H. The system approach to education. *Audiovisual Instruction,* 1968, *13*, 144-148.

Loughary, J.W. Instructional systems: Magic or method? *Educational Leadership,* 1968, *25*, 730-734.

Maccia, E.A., and Maccia, G.S. *Development of educational theory derived from three educational theory models.* Columbus: Ohio State University, 1966.

Mansergh, G.G. (Ed.) *A systems approach to student personnel services.* Detroit: Metropolitan Detroit Bureau of School Studies, Inc., 1969.

Meals, D.W. Heuristic models for systems planning. *Phi Delta Kappan,* 1967, *48*, 199-203.

Miller, D.R. *A system approach for solving educational*

problems. Burlingame, Calif.: Operation PEP, 1967.

Miller, R.I. Systems approach. *Educational Screen and Audiovisual Guide,* 1967, *46,* 28-29.

Nelson, J.L. Systems theory. *Social Education,* 1969, 225-227.

Oxhandler, K. Afterthoughts on a systems conference. *Audiovisual Instruction.* 1965, *10,* 395-397.

Pfeiffer, J., and Wilson, C.H. Do schoolmen have to learn systems analysis to survive? Review of new look at education. *Nations Schools,* 1969, *83,* 22.

Reisman, A. Higher education: A population flow feedback model. *Science,* 1966, *153,* 89.

Rowntree, D. Beyond programmes. *Times Educational Supplement,* 1968, 2766.

Ruark, H.C. IMC, systems approach, allies or adversaries? *Educational Screen and Audiovisual Guide,* 1966, *45,* 19.

Ruark, H.C. Multi-media method and the systems approach. *Educational Screen and Audiovisual Guide,* 1967, *46,* 21.

Silvern, L.C. A general system model of public education K-12. *Educational Technology,* 1964, *4,* 1-20.

Silvern, L.C. Cybernetics and education K-12. *Audiovisual Instruction,* 1968, *13,* 267-272.

Swanson, B.E. *Decision making in the school desegregation-decentralization controversies.* Center for Continuing Education and Community Studies. Bronxville, New York: Sarah Lawrence College, 1969.

Theobald, R. Higher education and cybernation. *NEA Journal,* 1966, *55* (3), 1966.

Thorson, S.D. Systems analysis and public education. *Journal of Secondary Education,* 1968, *42,* 243-266.

Tirrell, J.E. Total independent study at Oakland: Oakland Community College in Michigan seeks to develop a new learning model. *Junior College Journal,* 1966, *36,* 21-23.

Tondow, M. Systems analysis and innovation. *Journal of Secondary Education,* 1967, *42,* 261-266.

Van Dusseldorp, R.A. Systems approach. *NEA Journal,* 1967, *56,* 24-26.

Winthrop, H. Contemporary intellectual ferment and the curriculum of the future: General systems theory. *Social Studies,* 1965, *56,* 84.

Witherspoon, J.P. Educational communications systems: A whole problem look at transmission requirements of education. *Audiovisual Instruction,* 1966, *11,* 10-12.

Yee, A.H. Teacher education: Rube Goldberg or systems management? *Educational Technology,* 1969, *9* (9), 36-41.

Yee, A.H. Becoming a teacher. *Quest Monograph,* 1972, *28,* in press.

Systems Applications in Instruction

Anderson, R. The instructional systems approach. *Business Education World,* 1967, *47,* 6, 19.

Banathy, B.H. *Instructional Systems.* Palo Alto, Calif.: Fearon, 1968.

Barson, J. Heuristics of instructional systems development: A team report. *Audiovisual Instruction,* 1967, *12,* 613-614.

Barson, J., and Oxhandler, E.K. Systems: An approach to improving instruction. *Audiovisual Instruction,* 1965, *10,* 360.

Bratten, J.E. *The organization of a course for individual progress at Theodore High School—system analysis and simulation.* Santa Monica, Calif.: System Development Corporation, 1966.

Butler, F.C. *Instructional systems development for vocational and technical training.* Englewood Cliffs, N.J.: Educational Technology Publications, 1971.

Canfield, A.A. Instructional systems development. *Educational Screen and Audiovisual Guide*, 1967, *46*, 28-29.

Ciancone, E.S. New technique for instructional analysis. *Industrial Arts and Vocational Education*, 1968, *57*, 35-39.

Cogswell, J.F. *Nova High School—system analysis.* Santa Monica, Calif.: System Development Corporation, 1966.

Cooley, W.W., and Glaser, R. *An information and management system for individually prescribed instruction.* Working paper 44. Pittsburgh: Learning Research and Development Center, University of Pittsburgh, 1968.

Coulson, J.E. *Progress report for the instructional management system, May 10, 1968.* Santa Monica, Calif.: System Development Corp., 1968.

Drumheller, S.J. *Handbook of curriculum design for individualized instruction—A systems approach.* Englewood Cliffs, N.J.: Educational Technology Publications, 1971.

Eraut, R. An instructional systems approach to course development. *Audiovisual Communications Review*, 1967, *15*, 92-101.

Fishell, K.N. NDEA: Instructional systems approach at Syracuse. *Audiovisual Instruction*, 1966, *11*, 808.

Fritz, J.O. Emergence of instructional systems: The educationist's predicament. *Canadian Educational Research Digest*, 1968, *8*, 119-132.

Geddes, C.L., and Kooi, B.Y. Instructional management system for classroom teachers. *Elementary School Journal*, 1969, *69*, 337-345.

Gibson, T.L. Instructional systems design through in-service education. *Audiovisual Instruction*, 1968, *13*, 710-714.

Gilpin, J. Design and evaluation of instructional systems. *Audiovisual Communications Review*, 1962, *10*, 75-84.

Harey, J.B., *et al.* Heuristic dimension of instructional

development. *Audiovisual Communications Review,* 1968, *16,* 358-371.

Heinich, R. *The system engineering of education II: Application of systems thinking to instruction.* Los Angeles: University of Southern California, 1965.

Heinich, R. Application of systems concepts to instruction. *American Association for the Deaf,* 1966, *111,* 603-616.

Johnson, B.L. *Conference on systems approaches to curriculum and instruction in the open-door college.* Los Angeles: University of California, January 1967.

Joyce, B.R. Development of teaching strategies. *Audiovisual Instruction,* 1968, *13,* 820-827.

Knirk, F.G. Analysis of instructional systems: A reaction to the May issue. *Audiovisual Instruction,* 1965, *10,* 648-649.

MacDonald, J.B., and Wolfson, B.J. A case against behavioral objectives. *Elementary School Journal,* 1970, *71,* 119-128.

Mood, A.M. On some basic steps in the application of systems analysis to instruction. *Socio-Economic Planning Sciences,* 1967, *1,* 19-26.

Morgan, R.M. A review of developments in instructional technology. *Florida Journal of Educational Research,* 1964, *11,* 93-112.

Niedermeyer, F.C. *Developing exportable teacher training for criterion-referenced instructional programs.* Ingelwood, Calif.: Southwest Regional Laboratory, 1971.

Office of Economic Opportunity. *Instructional systems development manual.* Washington: Office of Economic Opportunity, Document number JCH 440.4, 1968.

Phillips, M.G. Learning materials and their implementation: The instructional systems concept. *Review of Educational Research,* 1966, *36,* 374.

Richardson, R.J. Information system for individualized instruction in an elementary school. *Education and Psychological Measurement,* 1969, *29,* 199-201.

Schalock, H.D., and Hale, J.R. (Eds.) *A competency based, field centered, systems approach to elementary teacher education, volume 1: Overview and specifications. Final report.* Portland, Northwest Regional Educational Laboratory, 1968.

Silberman, H.F. *Design objectives of the Instructional Management System.* Santa Monica, Calif.: System Development Corp., 1968.

Smith, R.G. *The design of instructional systems.* Technical Report No. 66-18. Alexandria, Virginia: Human Resources Research Office, George Washington University, 1966.

Stolurow, L.M. Some educational problems and prospects of a systems approach to instruction. Paper presented at Conference on New Dimensions for Research in Educational Media Implied by the "Systems" Approach to Instruction, Syracuse University, April 1964.

Tosti, D.T., and Ball, J.R. Behavioral approach to instructional design and media selection. *Audiovisual Communications Review,* 1969, *17,* 5-25.

Watson, P.G. Instructional strategies and learning systems. *Audiovisual Instruction,* 1968, *13,* 842-846.

Wayne, E.R. V.T.R.S.: An instructional system. *Audiovisual Instruction,* 1966, *11,* 752.

Yee, A.H., Shores, J., and Skuldt, K. Systematic flow-charting of educational objectives and process. *Audiovisual Communications Review,* 1970, *18,* 72-83.

Computer-Based Instructional Systems

Anderson, R.C., Kulhavy, R.W., and Andre, T. Feedback procedures in programmed instruction. A paper presented to the annual convention of the American Educational Research Association, March 1970.

Atkinson, R.C., and Wilson, H.A. *Computer-assisted instruction: A book of readings.* New York: Academic Press, 1969.

Baker, F.B. Automation of test scoring, reporting, and analysis. In R.L. Thorndike (Ed.), *Educational Measurement.* Chapter 8. Washington, D.C.: American Council on Education, 1970.

Baker, F.B. Computer based instructional management systems: A first look. *Review of Educational Research,* 1971, *41*, 1, 51-70.

Bisco, R.L. (Ed.) *Data bases, computer, and the social sciences.* New York: Wiley, 1970.

Bitzer, D.L., Lyman, E.R., and Easley, J.A. The uses of PLATO: Computer controlled teaching system. *Audiovisual Instruction,* 1966, *11*, 16-21.

Brudner, H.J. Computer-managed instruction. *Science,* 1968, *162*, 970-976.

Bundy, R.F. (Ed.) *Bibliography on computer-assisted instruction.* University of Rochester, New York: Clearinghouse on Self-Instructional Materials for Health Care Facilities, 1966.

Bushnell, D.D., and Allen, D.W. *The computer in American education.* New York: John Wiley and Sons, 1967.

Bushnell, D.D., and Cogswell, J.F. Computer-based laboratory for automation in school systems. *Audiovisual Communications Review,* 1961, *9*, 173-185.

Carter, L.F., and Silberman, H.F. The systems approach, technology and the school. Santa Monica, Calif.: System Development Corp., 1965. Report SP-2025, 1965.

Chesin, J.A. Teaching spelling by computer. *Minnesota Journal of Education,* 1967, *47*, 14-15.

Cogswell, J.F. Systems analysis and computer simulation in

the implementation of media. *Audiovisual Instruction,* 1965, *10,* 384-386.

Cogswell, J.F., *et al.* Construction and use of the school simulation vehicle. Santa Monica, Calif.: System Development Corp., 1964.

Cogswell, J.F. *et al.* Analysis of instructional systems. Report of a project, new solutions to implementing instructional media through analysis and simulation of school organization. Final report. Abstract No. ED 010 577. *Research in Education,* 1967.

Cogswell, J.F., and Estavan, D.P. Exploration in computer-assisted counseling. Santa Monica, Calif.: System Development Corp., 1965.

Cooley, W.W., and Glaser, R. An information and management system for individually prescribed instruction. In R.C. Atkinson and H.A. Wilson (Eds.), *Computer-assisted instruction: A book of readings.* New York: Academic Press, 1969.

DeVault, M.V., Kriewall, T.E., Buchanan, A.E., and Quilling, M.R. *Teacher's manual: Computer management for individualized instruction in mathematics and reading.* Unpublished manuscript of the Research and Development Center for Cognitive Learning, University of Wisconsin, 1969.

Easley, J.A., Jr. *A project to develop and evaluate a computerized system for instructional response analysis: Project SIRA. Final report.* Urbana: Computer-based Education Laboratory, University of Illinois, 1968.

Edgerton, A.K., and Twombly, R.M. A programmed course in spelling. *Elementary School Journal,* 1962, *62,* 380-386.

Finney, J.C. Methodological problems in programmed composition of psychological test reports. *Behavioral Science,* 1967, *12,* 142-152.

Fishman, E.J., Keller, L., and Atkinson, R.C. Massed vs. distributed practice in computerized spelling drills. *Journal of Educational Psychology,* 1968, *59,* 290-296.

Flanagan, J.C. Functional education for the seventies: Project PLAN. *Phi Delta Kappan,* 1967, *49,* 27-33.

Freiberger, W.F., and Prager, W. (Eds.) *Applications of digital computers.* New York: Ginn, 1963.

Fremer, J., and Anastasio, E.J. Computer-assisted item writing I (Spelling Items). *Journal of Educational Measurement,* 1969, *6* (2), 69-74.

Friedman, M.I. Effectiveness of machine instruction in the teaching of second and third grade spelling. *Journal of Educational Research,* 1967, *60,* 366-369.

Gentile, R.G. The first generation of computer-assisted instructional systems: An evaluative review. *Audiovisual Communications Review,* 1967, *15* (1), 23-53.

Harnack, R.S. Computer-based resource units in school situations. A special report of the Center for Curriculum Planning, Faculty of Educational Studies, State University of New York at Buffalo, 1969.

Howard, W.E. *"Individualized" schooling seen with computer.* New York: Long Island Press, 1968.

Kahn, A.B. Simulated apprenticeship. A paper presented to the IFIP World Conference on Computer Education, March 1970.

Kelley, A.C. An experiment with TIPS: A computer aided instructional system for undergraduate education. *The American Economic Review,* 1968, *58,* 446-457.

Knutson, J. Spelling drills using a computer-assisted instructional system. Technical Report No. 112, Stanford University, Institute for Mathematical Studies in the Social Sciences, 1967.

Kopp, H.G. Applications of systems concepts to teaching the deaf. *American Annals of the Deaf,* 1966, *111,*

668-669.

Lehmann, H. Systems approach to education: Project ARIS-TOTLE. *Audiovisual Instruction*, 1968, *13*, 144-148.

Lewis, B.N., and Pask, G. The theory and practice of adaptive teaching systems. In R. Glaser (Ed.), *Teaching machines and programmed learning, II: Data and directions*. Washington, D.C.: National Education Association, Department of Audiovisual Instruction, 1965, 213-266.

Loughary, J.W., *et al.* Autocoun: A computer-based automated counseling simulation system. *Personnel and Guidance Journal*, 1966, *45*, 6-15.

Moss, C.R. Engineering economics. In H.E. Mitzel and H. Wodtke (Eds.), *The development and presentation of four different college courses by computer teleprocessing*. University Park, Pa.: Computer-Assisted Instruction Laboratory, Pennsylvania State University, 1965.

National Security Industrial Association Project ARISTOTLE Symposium. Washington, D.C., December, 1967.

Noble, G., and Gray, K. The impact of programmed instruction: A longitudinal attitude study. *Programmed Learning and Educational Technology* (London), 1969, *6*, 271-282.

Norfleet, M. *Systems analysis in student personnel services.* Kentucky: Morehead State University, 1968.

Personke, C.R., and Yee, A.H. *Comprehensive spelling instruction: Theory, research, and application.* Scranton: International Textbooks, 1970.

Razik, T.A. *The educational technology bibliography series, Volume 1: Programmed instruction and computer assisted instruction.* Englewood Cliffs, N.J.: Educational Technology Publications, 1971.

Ridgeway, J. Computer-tutor: Competition for public education? *Education Digest*, 1966, *32*, 7-10.

Sass, M.A. (Ed.) *Computer augmentation of human reason-*

ing. Washington: Spartan, 1965.

Schure, A. Educational escalation through systems analysis: Project ULTRA at New York Institute of Technology. *Audiovisual Instruction,* 1965, *10,* 371-377.

Silberman, H.F. Research on programmed instruction at SDC. *School Life,* 1963, *45,* 13-15.

Silberman, H.F. Applications of computers in education. *Programmed Learning and Educational Technology* (London), 1968, *5,* 7-17.

Silvern, L.C. *Systems analysis and synthesis in training and education.* A technical report of the Automated Education Commission, University of Southern California, 1965.

Smith, T.W. Development of a research-based and computer-assisted guidance system. *Educational Leadership,* 1968, *25,* 754-760.

Spinrad, R.J. Automation in the laboratory. *Science,* 1967, *158,* 55-60.

Stewart, J.R., Jr. Improving instruction in bookkeeping through the systems approach. *Business Education Forum,* 1966, *21,* 14-16.

Stolurow, L.M. *Computer-based instruction: Psychological aspects and systems conception of instruction.* Cambridge: Graduate School of Education, Harvard University, 1967.

Stolurow, L.M. Defects and needs: SOCRATES, a computer-based instructional system in theory and research. *Journal of Experimental Education,* 1968, *37,* 102-117.

Suppes, P. On using computers to individualize instruction. In D.D. Bushnell and D.W. Allen (Eds.), *The computer in American education.* New York: John Wiley, 1967.

Suppes, P., and Morningstar, M. Computer-assisted instruction. *Science,* 1969, *166,* 343-350.

Taylor, A.J. Those magnificent men and their teaching

machines. *Educational Forum,* 1972, *36,* 239-246.

Uttal, W.R. *Real time computers: Technique and applications in the psychological services.* New York: Harper & Row, 1968.

Weisgerber, R.A., and Rahmlow, H.F. Individually managed learning: Project PLAN. *Audiovisual Instruction,* 1968, *13,* 835-839.

Withrow, F.B. Mediated learning. *Volta Review,* 1968, *70,* 453-457.

Systems Application in Educational Administration

Alioto, R.F., and Jungher, J.A. *Operational PPBS for education.* New York: Harper and Row, 1971.

Andrew, G.M. *Information-decision systems in education.* Itasca, Ill.: F.E. Peacock, 1971.

Bux, W.E. Understanding data processing through the systems concept: The A-E-I-O-U factors of data processing. *Business Education Forum,* 1967, *21,* 5-7.

Center for Vocational and Technical Education. *Program, planning, budgeting systems for educators. Volume I: An instructional outline. Leadership series No. 18.* Columbus: Center for Vocational and Technical Education, Ohio State University, 1969.

Cogswell, J.F., and Marsh, D.G. *System design for a continuous progress school—computer simulation of autonomous scheduling procedures.* Santa Monica, Calif.: System Development Corp., 1966.

Cogswell, J.F., et al. *Construction and use of the school simulation vehicle.* Santa Monica, Calif.: System Development Corporation, 1964.

Cogswell, J.F., et al. *Analysis of instructional systems. Report of a project, new solutions to implementing instructional media through analysis and simulation of school organization. Final report.* Santa Monica, Calif.: System Development Corporation, 1966.

Cook, D.L. *Program evaluation and review technique: Applications in education.* U.S. Office of Education Cooperative Research Monograph, 1966, No. 17.

Cook, D.L. Better project planning and control through the use of system analysis and management techniques. Paper presented at the Symposium on Operations Analysis of Education, sponsored by the National Center for Educational Statistics, Washington, D.C., November 20-22, 1967.

Cook, D.L. The use of systems analysis and management techniques in program planning and evaluation. Paper presented at the Symposium on the Application of Systems Analysis and Management Techniques to Educational Planning in California, Chapman College, Orange, Calif., June 12-13, 1967.

Cramer, P., and Gilman, S. PPBS: What should the school dollar buy? *Educational Leadership,* 1972, *29,* 664-667.

Educational Service Bureau, Inc. *Systems planning in public education.* Arlington, Virginia: Administrative Leadership Service, Educational Service Bureau, Inc., 1968.

Egbert, R.L., and Cogswell, J.F. *System design for a continuous progress school: Part I.* Santa Monica, Calif.: System Development Corporation, 1964.

Exton, E. How will systems approach affect the role of school boards? *American School Board Journal,* 1967, *155,* 13-15.

Greenwood, F. Data processing and systems. *Journal of Business Education,* 1965, *41,* 15-16.

Haggart, S.A., *et al. Program budgeting for school district planning.* Englewood Cliffs, N.J.: Educational Technology Publications, 1972.

Hartley, H.J. *Educational planning-programming-budgeting: A systems approach.* Englewood Cliffs, N.J.: Prentice-

Hall, 1968.

Hartley, H.J. PPBS: Status and implications. *Educational Leadership*, 1972, *29*, 658-661.

Hills, R.J. The concept of system. Revision of paper presented at the annual meeting of the American Educational Research Association, New York, February 16, 1967.

Hodges, R.B. Businessmen comment on the office framework, systems, and procedures. *American Business Education*, 1960, *17*, 56-60.

Kahn, G. Study of systems and procedures. *Business Education World*, 1969, *49*, 16-17.

Knezevich, S.J. The systems approach to school administration: Some perceptions on the state of the art in 1967. Paper presented at the U.S. Office of Education Symposium on Operations Analysis of Education, November 19-22, 1967.

Koenig, H.E. *A systems model for management, planning, and resource allocation in institutions of higher education.* Final report. East Lansing: Division of Engineering Research, Michigan State University, 1968.

Mansergh, G.G. (Ed.) *Systems approaches to the management of public education.* Detroit: Metropolitan Detroit Bureau of School Studies, Inc., 1969.

McIsaac, D.N. A time-cost management system. Technical paper of the Wisconsin Information System, University of Wisconsin, Madison, 1969.

Novick, D. *Origin and history of program budgeting.* Santa Monica, Calif.: Rand Corporation, 1966.

Ohio State University Faculty. *Program Planning, Budgeting Systems for Educators.* Columbus, Ohio: Center for Vocational and Technical Education, 1969.

Place, I. Data processing: Systems analysis. *National Business Education Yearbook*, 1964, *2*, 107-121.

Scribner, J.D. A systems analysis of school board action. Paper presented at the American Educational Research Association, Chicago, February 17, 1966.

Simon, H.A. Management by machines: How much and how soon? *The Management Review,* 1960, *49,* 12-19, 68-80.

Smith, R.P. PPBS: Hazard or promise? *Educational Leadership,* 1972, *29,* 662-663.

Swanson, A.D. Cost-utility analysis and educational decision-making. In G.G. Mansergh (Ed.) *A systems approach to student personnel services.* Detroit: Metropolitan Detroit Bureau of School Studies, Inc., 1969.

Talmadge, H. An experimental study in curriculum engineering. Paper presented at the American Educational Research Association conference, Chicago, February 8-10, 1968.

Tanner, C.K. Techniques and application of educational systems analysis: PERT, linear programming and utility/cost sensitivity analysis. *Audiovisual Instruction,* 1969, *14,* 89-90.

Thoresen, C.E. The system approach and counselor training: Basic features and implications. A paper presented to the annual meeting of the American Educational Research Association, March, 1968.

Tonne, H.A. Systems approach: Old wine in new bottles? *Journal of Business Education,* 1967, *43,* 8-9.

Tracz, G.S. An overview of optimal control theory applied to educational planning. Paper presented at the annual meeting of the American Educational Research Association, Los Angeles, February 5-8, 1969.

Van Gigch, J.P., and Hill, R.E. *Using systems analysis to implement cost-effectiveness and program budgeting in education.* Englewood Cliffs, N.J.: Educational Technology Publications, 1972.

Watkins, L.A. Systems and procedures. *Journal of Business*

Education, 1960, *36,* 77-78.

Yoho, L.W. SNAP maps of educational responsibility in industrial education: Systems network analysis process. *Industrial Arts and Vocational Education,* 1965, *54,* 34-35.

Systems Applications in Other Fields

Bayliss, L.E. *Living control systems.* San Francisco: Freeman, 1966.

Bell, D.A. *Intelligent machines: An introduction to cybernetics.* New York: Blaisdell, 1962.

Bertalanffy, L. von. The theory of open systems in physics and biology. *Science,* 1950, *111,* 23-29.

Bray, H.G., and White, K. Organisms as physico-chemical machines. *New Biology,* 1954, *16,* 70-85.

Buckley, W. (Ed.) *Modern systems research for the behavioral scientist: A source book.* Chicago: Aldine, 1968.

Chernoff, H., and Moses, L.E. *Elementary decision theory.* New York: Wiley, 1959.

DiStefano, J.J. III, Stubberud, A.R., and Williams, I.J. *Schaum's outline of theory and problems of feedback and control systems.* New York: Schaum, 1967.

Easton, D. *Social science education consortium. Publication 104, a systems approach to political life.* Lafayette, Ind.: Purdue University, 1966.

Egler, F.E. Bertalanffian organismicism. *Ecology,* 1953, *34,* 443-446.

Flagle, C.C., Huggins, W.H., and Roy, R.H. (Eds.). *Operations research and systems engineering.* Baltimore: Johns Hopkins, 1960.

Frank, L.K., *et al.* Teleological mechanisms. *New York Academy of Science,* 1948, *50.*

Gilbert, E.N. Information theory after 18 years. *Science,* 1966, *152,* 320-326.

Gordon, C.J., Jr. *Introduction to mathematical structures.* Belmont, Calif.: Dickenson, 1967.

Haray, F., Norman, R.Z., and Cartwright, D. *Structural models: An introduction to the theory of directed graphs.* New York: Wiley, 1965.

Helvey, T.C. *The age of information—An interdisciplinary survey of cybernetics.* Englewood Cliffs, N.J.: Educational Technology Publications, 1971.

Hoban, C.F. OR and curriculum planning. *Audiovisual Instruction,* 1968, *13,* 263-266.

Lewis, D.A. *Inception, design, and implementation of a management information system.* Dissertation submitted to American University, Washington, D.C., 1967.

Magrabi, F.M. Models and model building. *Journal of Home Economics,* 1965, *57,* 633-637.

Mayr, E. The role of systematics in biology. *Science,* 1968, *159,* 595-599.

Mesarovic, M.D. *Systems research and design.* New York: Wiley, 1961.

Milsum, J.H. *Biological control systems analysis.* New York: McGraw-Hill, 1966.

National Academy of Sciences. *Systematic biology: Proceedings of Ann Arbor Conference, 1967.* Washington, D.C.: NAS publication No. 1692, 1969.

Norfleet, M. *A systems approach to student personnel services.* Morehead, Kentucky: Morehead State University.

Oppenheim, A.V. Mathematics of systems. *Science,* 1967, *157,* 1030-1031.

Quastler, H. (Ed.) *Information theory in biology.* Urbana: University of Illinois, 1955.

Raiffa, H. *Decision analysis: Introductory lectures on choices under uncertainty.* Reading, Mass.: Addison-Wesley, 1968.

Rescher, N. (Ed.) *The logic of decision and action.* Pittsburgh: University of Pittsburgh, 1967.

Savas, E.S. Cybernetics in City Hall. *Science,* 1970, *168,* 1066-1071.

Simon, H.A., and Newell, A. Heuristic problem solving: The next advance in operations research. *Operations Research,* 1958, 6, 1.

Sisson, R.L. *Applying operational analysis to urban educational systems: A working paper.* Philadelphia: Management Science Center, University of Pennsylvania, January 6, 1967.

Stacy, R.W., and Waxman, B. (Eds.) *Computers in biomedical research. Vol. 2.* New York: Academic Press, 1965.

Stevens, M.E. *Research and development in the computer and information sciences, Volume 3. Overall system design considerations—A selective literature review.* Washington, D.C.: U.S. Department of Commerce, National Bureau of Standards, NBS Mono. 113, Vol. 3, 1970.

Watt, E.F. (Ed.) *Systems analysis in ecology.* New York: Academic, 1966.

Werts, C.E. *The study of college environments using path analysis.* Evanston, Ill.: National Merit Scholarship Corporation, 1967.

Wiener, N. *Cybernetics.* New York: Wiley, 1948.

Zwicky, F. *Discovery, invention, research, through the morphological approach.* New York: Macmillan, 1969.

Futuristic Viewpoints

Bell, D. The year 2000: The trajectory of an idea. *Daedalus,*

1967, *96*, 639-651.

Bell, D. The study of the future. *The Public Interest*, 1965, *1*, 119-130.

Boguslaw, W. *The new utopians*. Englewood Cliffs, N.J.: Prentice-Hall, 1965.

Brzezinski, Z. America and the technetronic age. *Encounter*, 1968a, *30*, 16-26.

Brzezinski, Z. Toward a technetronic society. *Current*, 1968b, *92*, 33-38.

Clarke, A.C. *Profiles of the future*. New York: Bantam, 1964a.

Clarke, A.C. *2001: A space odessey*. New York: Signet, 1964b.

Huxley, A. *Brave new world*. New York: Doubleday, Doran, 1932.

Huxley, A. *Brave new world revisited*. New York: Harper and Row, 1958.

Kahn, H., and Wiener, A.J. *The year 2000*. New York: Macmillan, 1967.

Orwell, G. *1984*. New York: Harcourt, Brace, 1949.

Skinner, B.F. *Walden two*. New York: Macmillan, 1962.

Weinberg, A.M. Can technology replace social engineering? *University of Chicago Magazine*, 1966, *49*, 6-10.

Weinberg, A.M. Can technology stabilize world order? *Public Administration Review*, 1967, *27*, 460-464.

Perspective Viewpoints

Apple, M.W. Behaviorism and conservatism. In B.R. Joyce and M. Weil (Eds.), *Prospectives for reform in teacher education*. Englewood Cliffs, N.J.: Prentice-Hall, 1972.

Arendt, H. *The human condition*. New York: Doubleday Anchor, 1958.

Armytage, W.H.G. *The rise of the technocrats.* London: Routledge and Kegan Paul, 1965.

Baram, M.S. Social control of science and technology. *Science,* 1971, *172,* 535-539.

Bertalanffy, L. von. Philosophy of science in scientific education. *Scientific Monthly,* 1953, 77, 233.

Boffey, P.M. Systems analysis: No panacea for nation's domestic problems. *Science,* 1967, *158,* 1028-2030.

Brooks, H., and Poers. R. The assessment of technology. *Scientific American,* 1970, *222* (2), 13-21.

Churchman, C.W. *Challenge to reason.* New York: McGraw-Hill, 1968.

Colodny, R.G. (Ed.), *Mind and cosmos: Essays in contemporary science and philosophy.* Pittsburgh: University of Pittsburgh Press, 1966.

Davis, R.H. The advance to cybernation: 1965-1985. In R. Theobald (Ed.), *The guaranteed income.* New York: Anchor, 1967.

Demerath, N.J., III, and Peterson, R.A. (Eds.) *System, change, and conflict: A reader on contemporary sociological theory and the debate over functionalism.* New York: Free Press, 1967.

Ellul, J. *The technological society.* New York: Vintage, 1964.

Ellul, J. *The political illusion.* New York: Knopf, 1968.

Ferkiss, V.C. *Technological man: The myth and the reality.* New York: Mentor, 1969.

Ferry, W.H. Must we rewrite the Constitution to control technology? *Saturday Review,* 1968, *51* (9), 50-54.

Fromm, E. *The revolution of hope: Toward a humanized society.* New York: Bantam, 1968.

Goodman, P. *People or personnel.* New York: Vintage Books, 1968.

Goodman, P. Can technology be humane? In M. Brown (Ed.), *The social responsibility of the scientist.* New York:

Free Press, 1971, 247-265.

Goran, M. The literati revolt against science. *Philosophy of Science*, 1940, *7*, 379-384.

Habermas, J. Knowledge and interest. In D. Emmet and A. MacIntyre (Eds.), *Sociological theory and philosophical analysis.* New York: Macmillan, 1970.

Jones, R.D. (Ed.), *Unity and diversity.* New York: Braziller, 1969.

Koestler, A. *The ghost in the machine.* New York: Macmillan, 1968.

McLuhan, M. *The mechanical bride.* New York: Vanguard, 1951.

McLuhan, M. *Understanding media.* New York: McGraw-Hill, 1965.

Mumford, L. *Technics and civilization.* New York: Harcourt, Brace, 1934.

Mumford, L. *The culture of cities.* New York: Harcourt, Brace, 1938.

Mumford, L. Utopia, the city and the machine. *Daedalus,* 1965, *94,* 271-292.

Mumford, L. *The myth of the machine.* New York: Harcourt, Brace, 1967.

Oettinger, A., and Marks, S. Educational technology: New myths and old realities. *Harvard Educational Review,* 1968, *38,* 697-717.

Oppenheimer, J.R. Analogy in science. *American Psychologist,* 1956, *11,* 127-135.

Parker, E.G., and Dunn, D.A. Information technology: Its social potential. *Science,* 1972, *176,* 1392-1399.

Rosenblueth, A., and Wiener, N. The role of models in science. *Philosophy of Science,* 1945, *12,* 315-321.

Schou, D.A. *Technology and change.* New York: Delacorte, 1967.

Sennett, R. *The uses of disorder.* New York: Vintage, 1970.

Skinner, B.F. Freedom and the control of man. *American Scholar*, 1955-56, *25*, 45-65.

Sorokin, P.A. *Sociological theories of today.* New York: Harper and Row, 1966.

Veblen, T. *The place of science in modern civilization and other essays.* New York: B.W. Huebsel, 1919.

Concluding Comments

The fact that educational systems management is an emerging science is reflected clearly in the literature of the field. Very few scholars who would apply concepts from general systems theory or the more established systems sciences have attempted to justify such applications. While pragmatic and utilitarian arguments abound in the literature, serious inquiry into the appropriateness of systems applications in education is found almost solely in the work of its critics.

Most proponents of educational systems management attempt to apply established systems sciences, such as cybernetics, without full extrapolation to the field of education. As justification for such applications is almost never fully presented, systems applications have effectively divided the educational populace into conflicting camps without providing a common basis for intellectual debate. If those who support the use of systems applications would address themselves to substantive issues regarding the moral, ethical, sociological, and psychological effects of educational systems management, they would open the door to more rigorous and meaningful analysis of their adopted techniques. This conceptual analysis of the goodness-of-fit of systems applications to educational concepts will require a great deal of effort. However, without such analysis the fledgling field will be unable to win greater acceptance among curriculum theorists and will continue to be rejected by those who might otherwise benefit from its organizational and analytical potential.

The need for new educational techniques based on general systems theory is more crucial than the need for justification of existing systems applications in the field. To date, the only application of systems concepts in education has been the description and analysis of closed systems. Closed systems are composed of finite inputs, operations, and output. Within such systems, the general systems properties of differentiation of roles among the components, progressive mechanization of the operations, and the increased specification or regulation of the system's functions are greatly emphasized. Closed systems, being mechanistic sets of operations limited to applications in which the output may be specified in advance, may prove to have little relevance to the problems of education.

What is apparently needed in education are *systems which are capable of incorporating the generative nature of a human being into their structure.* Such systems would probably maximize the general systems properties of goal directedness, and multivariable interaction of component parts. Under the labels of "generative" and "living" systems, open systems have been developed from general systems theory in biology and physics. While such models seemingly lack some of the precision inherent in closed systems, they have been shown to more adequately account for the roles played by biological organisms and physical phenomena. If similar models can be described and analyzed in education, many significant problems regarding the roles of concepts and people within the process of education might be addressed.

The developments of new techniques for educational systems management may not be found by critical analysis of existing techniques. While the applications of open systems must be carefully examined for their possible incorporation into education, it is essential that the concept of general systems itself be scrutinized to determine the relationship between its precepts and educational concepts. If those familiar with the needs of education conduct a thorough analysis of the existing literature on general systems theory, techniques may be developed which are more directly applicable to the field of education. Until the difficult task of relating technique and procedure to educational need and function is undertaken and greater dialogue is established between systems analysts and educators, educational systems management will not become a legitimate systems science and a productive asset to education.

ABOUT THE AUTHORS

Michael W. Apple is Assistant Professor of Curriculum and Instruction at the University of Wisconsin, Madison. He received his masters and doctorate from Teachers College, Columbia University, where he studied philosophy and curriculum theory and development. He recently co-authored *Implementing Systems Models for Teacher Education.* His major interests include curriculum theory, the problem of ideology and curriculum thought, and "the hidden curriculum."

W. James Popham is Professor of Education, University of California, Los Angeles. He earned a B.A. and M. Ed. from the University of Portland and an Ed.D. from Indiana University. His many publications include: *The Teacher Empiricist, Criterion-Referenced Measurement, Systematic Instruction,* and *Educational Statistics: Use and Interpretation.* Dr. Popham is Director of the Instructional Objectives Exchange and is 1972 Vice President of Division D, Measurement and Research Methodology, of the American Educational Research Association. He received the AERA-American Educational Publications Association award in 1971 for outstanding research contributions to the development of educational materials. He is currently involved in the development of criterion-referenced tests for school evaluation and studying the suitability of performance tests to estimate pre- and in-service teaching proficiency.

Albert H. Yee is Professor of Curriculum and Instruction at the University of Wisconsin at Madison. He received a B.A. from the University of California, Berkeley; an M.A. from San Francisco State College; an Ed.D. from Stanford; and completed a USOE post-doctoral research fellowship at the University of Oregon. His publications include *Social Interaction in Educational Settings* and co-authorship of *Comprehensive Spelling Instruction: Theory, Research, and Application.* His major research interest is in the social psychology of education, which he was invited to present as Senior Fulbright-Hays Lecturer at the University of Tokyo, Tamagawa University, and other Japanese universities, 1972. Among his current projects: a textbook on interdisciplinary approaches in educational research, statistical techniques to study causal inferences, and cross-cultural aspects of social interaction in education.

Louis Fischer is Professor of Education, University of Massachusetts, Amherst. His undergraduate work was at Ohio State University and he holds M.A., LL.B. and Ph.D. degrees from Stanford University. His teaching experience includes the primary, upper elementary and secondary grades as well as higher education. His primary interests are in philosophy of education, social foundations of education, and civil rights and education. Currently he is editing a series of books on crucial issues in education, with Harper & Row, Publishers, Inc., and is director of the Center of Educational Foundations at the University of Massachusetts.

Robert Sinclair for the past five years has worked to initiate quality education in classrooms, schools, and school systems across the country. Professor Sinclair's present efforts include integration of the schools in Montclair, New Jersey; initiation of open education in the rural school setting of Rockingham County, Virginia; and implementation of a massive six-year staff leadership program in Prince William County, Virginia.

Sinclair's work with actual problems is complemented by research in how children perceive educational environments in elementary schools. An instrument, *Elementary School Environment Survey*, was developed by Sinclair to report conditions in schools as seen through the eyes of children. Dr. Sinclair is also inquiring into how teachers view their own power to cause change in schools, and creating a procedure for teachers to develop emergent curriculum.

Dr. Sinclair is presently Director of the Program in Curriculum Studies at the University of Massachusetts.

Jay H. Shores is an Assistant Professor at the University of Houston. He received a B.S. and M.S. from the University of Illinois at Urbana and his Ph.D. at the University of Wisconsin at Madison. His major research and writing interest is in educational systems management.